BEN LAW is a writer, woodsman, carpenter and eco-builder. He has lived and worked in Prickly Nut Wood in West Sussex for over twenty years, in his unique home, the building which was filmed for Channel 4's *Grand Designs* and was voted by viewers the most popular Grand Design ever. His authentic, incredible sense of the land and the wildlife, and his respect for age-old traditions and how to sustain them offers a wonderful, inviting insight into the life and character of Prickly Nut Wood.

Praise for Ben Law:

'You couldn't find a house that has a more intimate relationship with people and place.' KEVIN MCCLOUD

'A fascinating chronicle of a dream'

Good Woodworking

'This book will leave you with a sense of awe and admiration but also a yearning to follow in Ben's footsteps.' *Permaculture* magazine

'A vi

lwoods

Woodsman

LIVING IN A WOOD IN THE 21st CENTURY

Ben Law

Illustrations by Jane Bottomley

WILLIAM COLLINS

William Collins
An imprint of HarperCollins*Publishers*
77–85 Fulham Palace Road
London W6 8JB

WilliamCollinsBooks.com

This William Collins paperback edition published 2014

20 19 18 17 16 15 14
10 9 8 7 6 5 4 3 2 1

First published in Great Britain by Collins in 2013

Text © Ben Law 2013
Illustrations © Jane Bottomley

Ben Law asserts the moral right to
be identified as the author of this work

A catalogue record for this book
is available from the British Library

ISBN 978-0-00-755192-7

Printed and bound in Great Britain by
Clays Ltd, St Ives plc

MIX
Paper from
responsible sources
FSC® C007454

FSC™ is a non-profit international organisation established to promote
the responsible management of the world's forests. Products carrying the
FSC label are independently certified to assure consumers that they come
from forests that are managed to meet the social, economic and
ecological needs of present and future generations,
and other controlled sources.

Find out more about HarperCollins and the environment at
www.harpercollins.co.uk/green

Contents

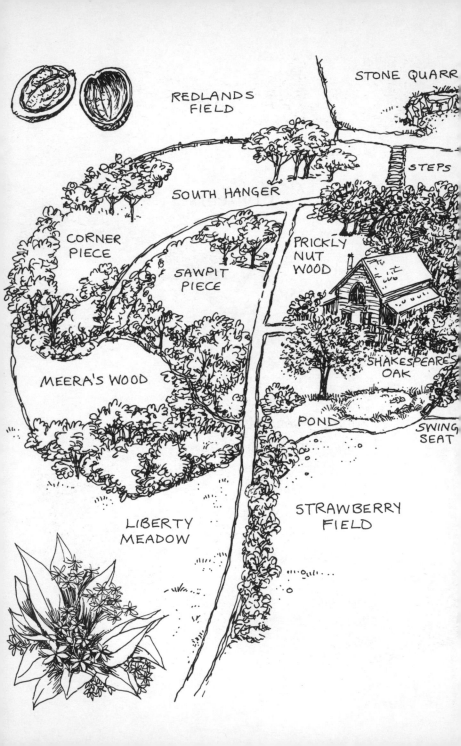

STONE QUARR

REDLANDS
FIELD

STEPS

SOUTH HANGER

CORNER
PIECE

PRICKLY
NUT
WOOD

SAWPIT
PIECE

MEERA'S WOOD

SHAKESPEARES
OAK

POND

SWING
SEAT

LIBERTY
MEADOW

STRAWBERRY
FIELD

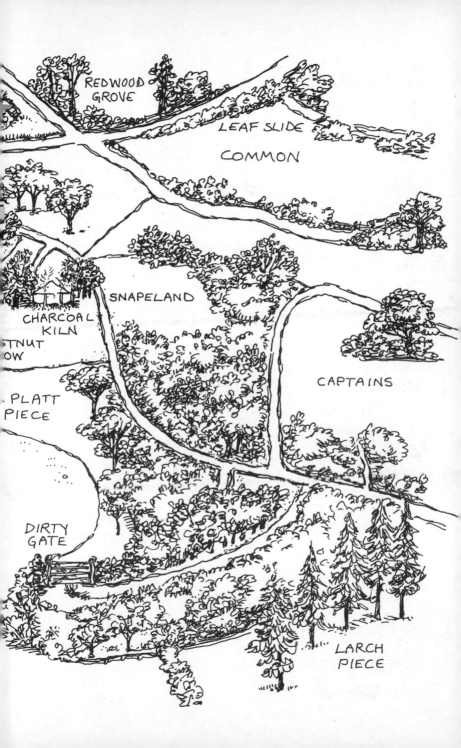

REDWOOD GROVE

LEAF SLIDE

COMMON

CHARCOAL KILN

SNAPELAND

TNUT OW

PLATT PIECE

CAPTAINS

DIRTY GATE

LARCH PIECE

For my children
Rowan, Zed and Tess

– CHAPTER ONE –

Woodland Immersion

'I know this place. I belong.'

I am standing within this place I know as Prickly
Nut Wood, and deep from within my belly I send
a deer bark, throaty with a characteristic rasp. I emit
it with focus and penetration in response to a roe stag
who challenges my territory.

Such behaviour might sound strange or perhaps
alarming, yet I belong here not just as a human being
amongst other human beings but as a mammal
amongst the inhabitants of this forest.

I have been living within Prickly Nut Wood for
twenty years now and I can make the bold statement
'I know this place' through my learning and observation of this environment. It has taken twenty years
and I will know it better in another twenty. 'I belong'
comes not purely from the passage of time but also

from my integration into the world of this forest. As a forest dweller and dominant mammal, I have immersed myself in the heartbeat of this woodland, its diversity and seasonal changes, and have acquired an altered sense of time and a deep knowledge of the detail of the landscape.

*   *   *

My early years here were quiet and luxurious, allowing me time for observation and reflection. My first dwelling, a simple structure built from bent hazel sticks and canvas, nestled discreetly within the forest flora. I was new to this world – I arrived, listened and observed, absorbing my new surroundings. I had neither radio nor telephone, nor any form of communication with the world beyond Prickly Nut Wood, save my own legs to carry me away from it for provisions and occasional human contact.

There was no road or track into Prickly Nut Wood. I would walk in along a footpath that twisted through steep banks of beech and yew and passed visible remnants of small earth banks that once enclosed the field system of people now long departed. Each bank, rich in mosses and ferns, and the occasional remains of a sandstone wall, can be made out along the pathway. The footpath climbs up into heavier soils, where the beech gives way to oak and sweet chestnut, and after winter rains the path too becomes heavy underfoot. My first journey is challenging – I look for obvious landmarks, a big oak here, a fallen chestnut there. These are the signposts that will help me find my way in and out of my chosen world.

As time passes the path becomes familiar. I notice smaller trees, subtleties on a stone half hidden in the wood bank; a wren building its mossy nest in a crevice in a chestnut stump becomes familiar, and as I walk back and forth I observe its busy life being acted out for me, its sole audience. I listen out for the chicks and watch the continual supplies of food being flown into the moss-lined hole, as if the bird were a pilot dropping food parcels in time of famine to desperate, waiting human beings. One day as I pass by, all is quiet. The wrens have fledged and departed. Was I the only person who knew of their whereabouts?

By now the large trees that were once my signposts are in the background. I am aware of passing them but no longer need their reassurance for my sense of direction.

Where the footpath borders Prickly Nut Wood, the escarpment is steep and falls away into the labyrinth of forest tracks amongst the dense coppiced sweet chestnut of the wood. I attached a rope at the top in the early days to help me scramble up and down the hill, as at that time it was my only way in. Over the years, I have carved out steps and my days of sliding through a muddy river cascading down the hillside are past, but the sense of adventure and the feeling of being totally alive in the woodland world as I make my way back instinctively to my home have not disappeared.

The Great Storm of 1987 swept through Prickly Nut Wood but the hill to the south-west helped baffle many of the areas of coppice from the power of the wind and only some of the taller trees were uprooted. The coppice stems, more flexible on their sturdy stumps, could blow and spring back again. One large sweet chestnut that was uprooted by the storm continues to grow in the way that chestnut will, sending up vertical stems from what was once the main stem, which now lies horizontal across the woodland floor. The new shoots have grown up and lean forwards towards the light, creating a canopy. It was under this canopy that I lit my first fire in the wood.

This fire marked my arrival and I stayed with it until the last of the day had gone. Curled up on a March evening around the embers, I listened for the first time to Prickly Nut Wood at night. The woodland awoke as the darkness drew in, and I heard the hooting of a tawny owl, followed by the familiar 'kee-wick' note resonating crisply in the chill of the evening. Soon there was a cacophony of owls conversing with one another, filling the wood with their invisible presence. After some time it stilled to a momentary silence. I could hear my gentle pulse of breath. Then, a scurrying and rustle of the leaves. I now recognise the sound of a mouse on chestnut leaves in March, but twenty years ago it was unknown to me, and it was near. It was followed by a crackle and a noise that made me freeze – a roe stag let out its territorial bark, deep and primal, and then the scraping and stamping of its hoof. I felt vulnerable, a horizontal figure wrapped around the glowing embers of the fire. I was within the territory of another and felt as a trespasser must feel when confronted by an angry landowner, shotgun in hand. The next bark resounded further away, and I relaxed my breathing and allowed my eyes to close once again.

I awoke cold but filled with an overwhelming sense of arrival. The first shafts of light highlighted the crisp lace that lay across the surrounding chestnut leaves, and the sound of awakening birds grew until the volume and variety became so intermingled that it became hard to discern individuals amongst the masses. I pulled my blanket away from my face and engaged with the fresh feeling of pure cold that the icy air communicated in engaging with my skin. I surveyed the unfamiliar outlines of the chestnut trees and a large holly, whose evergreen presence was clear beyond the leafless chestnut stems. A warmth emanated from within me. I had arrived in the forest and I had much to learn.

*   *   *

Prickly Nut Wood is an area of less than eight acres of predominantly sweet chestnut coppice on the north-east face of a hill. The soil is greensand over Wealden clay, and springs break naturally between the soil layers, ensuring that the land is damp underfoot for much of the year. It was within this setting that I began my forest-dwelling life. Eight miles away, a busy railway station shipped the gathering flow of commuters into central London. But life at Prickly Nut Wood could not be further removed from such an environment.

A few more nights curled around the fireside embers and it was time to build my first home. I had made 'benders' from hazel poles at festivals when I was a teenager. Low-impact and quick to build, with the wooden resource growing all around me, it seemed the obvious structure to begin with. In fact, it remained my home for two years. I cut about thirty hazel stems about one inch in diameter and forced the butt ends into the ground. I pulled the tall tops down with a rope and then secured them to the pulled-down tops of the opposing poles, creating a series of hoops like a wooden polytunnel frame. I square-lashed them with sisal and hemp cord, and soon had the framework of my home. I already had some army surplus green canvas tarpaulins and these I lashed over the frame. I now had a shelter and over the coming months developed it into my home. I collected pallets to make a raised floor, an old woodburner to keep the bender dry and warm, and a window and frame from a skip to give me a view out into the woodland, so on the wettest of days I could look out and continue my observations from my warm, yet simple home.

For me, the period of observation was to help minimise mistakes I might otherwise have made in being too hasty and forcing my ideas on to an environment that I did not fully understand. It's all too easy to arrive with pre-conceived ideas about land we wish to work, and then start implementing them, unaware of the damage we may be doing to the established order. Prickly Nut Wood has been woodland for at least 400 years, although the ground flora and earthworks would suggest longer. Who was I in my short life to feel I knew better than 400+ years of established plant, insect and animal relationships? Part of my observation was to study these relationships and learn through the changing seasons the patterns and activities of resident and migratory species. To help with this I kept notes and diary entries, and made links between food plants, caterpillars and their butterflies and moths, and woodland management techniques that encouraged the right environment to allow these species the opportunity to continue to survive and thrive within Prickly Nut Wood.

27 May

I have been watching the dead top of a large chestnut tree. It has bothered me since I first arrived here as it looks unhealthy and stands out above the coppice with its dead crown. It stands out all the more now the leaf has broken and everywhere has greened up. But the more I watch it, the more I have noticed what a popular spot it is for birds. It seems to be a viewing post for all visiting birds to the wood. Last night its purpose as a marking post was clearly pointed out to me when the woodland came alive with the 'churring' sound of the nightjar. Having flown from his winter retreat in Africa he had returned and picked this dead top of the chestnut from which to make his presence known. After a few minutes he stopped 'churring', swooped down, clapped his wings together and made for the large oak before beginning 'churring' once again. He then chose a birch before returning to the dead top of the chestnut tree to make his final call, his territory now clearly marked.

Without my time of observation, I might have followed my first impulse and felled the chestnut tree with the dead top, and never known of its importance to the nightjar or other birds. We have little understanding of the roles of particular trees in the lives of birds but even basic observation shows us that they spend a lot more time in direct relationship to trees than we do. With the exception of a few groups of forest-dwelling people around the world, it is unusual for us to live in trees, while for many species of birds it is clearly their usual location.

Many of our woodlands in the UK are managed based on plans that have taken little time for detailed observation, and many habitats are lost because of this. It is common for felling licences to be applied for to fell trees within a woodland, with only one visit

having been carried out. If I had not been staying at Prickly Nut Wood at night, how would I have known that nightjars were migratory visitors to the land? The chances of seeing them in daytime are low, as they are highly camouflaged and stay on the ground. They do not create a proper nest, but scrape the ground and lay their eggs directly on to it.

My spring mornings would begin just before the awakening dawn chorus. On many mornings I would awake as the first glimmer of light brought form to the evolving silhouettes and wander over to the fire-pit and light a fire and put the kettle on.

Lighting a fire to boil water is a simple and satisfying experience, provided you are prepared and well stocked with firewood and kindling. My morning fire would begin with fine strips of birch bark, with small, dry twigs of sweet chestnut laid on top. I would light the fire and slowly blow into an old copper pipe with a flattened end, so as to direct my breath with good velocity wherever I pointed the pipe. As the fire took, I would build up the fire further with slightly larger pieces of chestnut. With stacks of dry material sorted into piles by their size, lighting a fire becomes as easy as turning on a cooker.

With the kettle on the fire, I would wait listening for the first sound to break the morning silence. I am still astonished how fast the chorus builds up. From the first delicate tones of the opening bird, within a couple of minutes there are so many birds singing that it becomes almost impossible to try to discern one bird from another. The dawn chorus in a broadleaf woodland in spring is truly one of the wonders of the world and a magical part of the environment I inhabit. Every year I am refreshingly amazed by its intensity of volume; friends who have stayed with me have resorted to ear defenders, so as not to be woken at 4.30 am. As for me, I am always happy to catch the first notes and will sometimes return to sleep after a brief ten-minute burst of choral bird song. To have such an array of birds within the woodland clearly shows that there is sufficient food and that it is an ideal habitat for them.

Observing the landscape of a woodland takes time. There is not the clear expanse of a grass field with hedgerows neatly marking the boundaries. A woodland offers little in the way of vistas to give you perspective of size or space. With an ancient woodland such as Prickly Nut Wood, which has not been cultivated by the plough and undulates across the landscape, much of the topography is hidden by the trees themselves. Added to this, Prickly Nut Wood had a thick wall of *Rhododendron ponticum*, which made the landscape impenetrable in places and further disguises the topography.

I remember clearly one of my first adventures, cutting a path through the rhododendron, bill hook in hand, and arriving suddenly at the base of a large oak tree. This tree, the largest in the wood, would stand out in any other landscape but here it was hidden amongst tall chestnut stems, birch re-growth and the blanket wall of established rhododendron. I estimate the tree to be around 300 to 350 years old, which is young to middle-aged for an oak tree. It has a circumference of more than 7 metres and a height of more than 25 metres. Its crown is similar to a parkland or field tree, in that it has spread and formed a large canopy. The regular cutting of the coppice woodland below it will have helped give it the light to expand and the coppice re-growth will have helped push the tree up taller. It stands proudly on a ridge and now I have cut the coppice to the north, the true branching pattern of the cerebral crown can be seen in its full glory. I have attached a swing seat to the oak and it makes a wonderful spot from which to survey the woodland and across to Blackdown beyond.

Having found the tree for the first time, I sat down on a mossy seat formed between the root buttresses and contemplated the changes that might have occurred during the life of a tree of this age. Perhaps germinating as a seed during the English Civil War, it will have been growing through countless changes, numerous wars and a good few king and queens. One of the buttresses has a large scar across it, angled as a woodsman would angle a cut to remove the buttress prior to setting the tree up for felling. The scar has calloused over and I like to think it was caused by a woodsman who, after beginning the cut, thought better of felling such a magnificent tree and decided to leave it to grow on. I am very thankful that he did.

It has also been struck by lightning on two occasions and carries the scars right down its trunk. The tree seems in good health and shows no signs of distress from this experience, bar the scars.

I often lie on the ground and look up through the vast array of branches, marvelling at the tree's ability to hold up such a huge weight of timber high into the sky, and then consider the volume of water the tree is absorbing and then pumping through the sap layer to reach the millions of little leaves high above.

I can only guess at the role and value this tree has played in the lives of others who have gone before me, but even in my twenty years at Prickly Nut Wood it has become a focal point for celebration and contemplation.

My eldest son Rowan has the ashes of his maternal grandfather scattered beneath the oak, its presence seeming fit to be the chosen resting place by his grandmother after the loss of her husband. Friends of mine have asked to come and sit beneath it when they are going through a troubled period in their lives or are just seeking a quiet space. I too have turned to the tree and used its calm, ancient and peaceful presence when I have had troubles of my own.

It has featured as a focal point in a production of Shakespeare's *A Midsummer Night's Dream*, and is referred to in the book *The Bard and Co*, in which the tree is named 'Shakespeare's Oak'. Its acorns were recently taken to the Globe Theatre in London and then distributed, along with a picture of the tree, to those who attended to take away and plant.

Yesterday, Ben Law introduced it to us, the oldest tree in the wood. At this time of year, the scattered acorns were sprouting and beginning to send roots into the ground. We collected several cupfuls with the aim of giving everyone an acorn from Shakespeare's Oak (now newly named).

The Bard and Co.

A local herbalist became a regular visitor to the oak tree. She was moved by the presence of 'tree spirits' that she clearly sensed when around the tree. Although I cannot claim to have had such an other-worldly experience, I am also drawn to the tree. Whether out of superstition or respect, in spring I always find myself looking across to the oak tree and subconsciously asking the tree's blessing to continue burning charcoal in the woods.

The tree has always been a magical place for my children. Zed and Tess know the tree as 'the story-telling tree', for when you sit on the bench suspended from its limbs and swing and ask the tree politely for a story about whatever you wish for, the tree always responds (with a little help) by telling a story.

There is no doubt in my mind that this tree has become a sacred place to me and my family and friends over the last 20 years, and whether by circumstance or unknown force we have all in our way been drawn by the presence of this magical, ancient tree.

Beyond the oak, the woodland drops away through more sweet chestnut coppice and comes to a stream that flows near the northern boundary. This stream picks up both surface run-off from the woodland and the escarpment above, and is also fed by the springs that break between the clay and greensand soil layers.

It opens out into a pond, now a wildlife haven for dragon- and damsel-flies, newts and often a grass snake.

7 May

Glorious day. I awoke to shafts of sunlight across my face and after a good stretch and a couple of cups of tea, I headed down to the pond for a swim. I slid in off the platform and as always was shocked by the icy-cool, spring-fed water. I had been treading water for a couple of minutes when a shape caught my attention. Turning towards it, I had the strange sensation of observing a grass snake swimming past me, just a couple of feet away and right in my line of sight. Its agility in the water was impressive and it made quickly for the far bank, disappearing amongst some flag iris.

Swimming in the pond became a morning ritual in my early years at Prickly Nut Wood. I built a small, wooden ladder and a few planks for a platform, and this allowed me to enter and exit the pond without my feet disturbing the muddy banks and clouding the clear water. The temperature of the water means a dip is usually just that, and most of my time is spent sitting on the platform observing the comings and goings in the pond.

The pond sits on the woodland edge, benefiting from the environment of the woodland on one side and the organic hay field on the other. Between the pond and the field, there is a narrow wood bank and a ditch. The ditch has been mechanically cleared many times but the bank retains its archaeological features. Wood banks were once common along the perimeter of ancient woodlands; the ditch would usually be on the outside of the wood, with the bank stretching some thirty feet back into the wood. The Prickly Nut wood bank seems narrow and may have been disturbed when the chestnut was planted some 130 to 150 years ago.

In spring the bank is abundant with primroses, bluebells and some early purple-flowering orchid. This diversity is also enhanced by the wood bank

being situated both at the edge of the wood and the edge of the field. The edge between two different landscapes attracts species from both forms of landscape, and species unique to the edge environment itself also colonise the bank, often making these edge habitats the most diverse habitats in our landscape.

I have now coppiced this area from the oak tree to the pond three times, and the biodiversity and abundance have increased with each cut. But it was all very different when I first stumbled across this area. My first experience involved battling through the twisted stems of rhododendron and I did not emerge by a beautiful dragonfly-dappled pond; to the contrary, I came out at a farm rubbish dump, full of rusty metal, cans of oil and old milk crates, through which grew a few self-seeded goat willows in a large indentation in the landscape that was once a pond. I loaded a trailer with this collection of dumped items and took them to be recycled. I then hired a digger and began the process of clearing out silt and willow roots until I met the seam of clay I knew would lie waiting to be used again. Clay will hold water naturally if it is 'puddled'. Puddling involves working the clay layer with one's feet until it becomes smooth and creamy, creating a seal across the surface of the clay. Pigs are often used, as they naturally puddle clay with their rooting and mud-creating habits. I didn't have a pig to do the puddling, but the excellent Wealden clay puddled up with the help of a little rain and a good amount of working between my feet. Puddling is quite labour-intensive but can be a fun social event if you pick a warm day, choose the right music and arrange a puddling party. Twenty or thirty people dancing Irish jigs in the mud at the bottom of a pond is a lot more fun than spreading out a butyl pond liner. Slowly, over the coming months, the pond began to refill until one day I noticed water lapping over the large stone I had placed in the overflow outlet. The water then flows into a network of streams until it finds the River Lod, flows on into the River Rother, then on into the River Arun and eventually out to sea at Littlehampton. With the pond naturally filled, it did not take long for the biodiversity to increase and the pond to become the haven for wildlife that it is today.

Storing water has to be one of the most practical ways we can improve and help our local environment. I am astonished how much rainwater it is possible to catch, even off a modest-sized roof. When I lived for a couple of years in a 30- by 10-foot caravan, I collected the rainwater off the roof in four 50-gallon rainwater butts that were all linked together. The butts were raised up and I drew the water off the end butt through the caravan wall and out through a tap into the sink. These butts supplied all the water I needed for washing up and to run a shower throughout the whole year. Even when they began to run low in summer, it took just one big thunderstorm and they were all filled up again.

If you measure the area of the roof of your house and multiply it by the average local rainfall for your area (available from your local meteorological office) you will be able to estimate the average volume of rainwater you could be collecting from your roof. I have two buried 10,000-litre tanks that irrigate all the vegetable gardens and that are often overflowing. You will most likely be surprised to find how much water you could be harvesting from your roof.

It is easy to become complacent in England about water, as often we have lots of it. But droughts are not uncommon, and as our climate seems unpredictable and unsettled it would make sense for every home to be maximising their water-storage options. It should be compulsory for every new home to have water storage as part of the design.

*   *   *

My first year at Prickly Nut Wood was one of observation. Of course, I cut wood, built myself a basic shelter and drew water from an old catchment well within the woods, but beyond that I came to observe.

It was the late 1980s and I had been travelling in South America, predominantly searching for solutions to the leaflets that kept appearing through the letterbox telling me an area of the Amazon rainforest the size of Belgium was being destroyed every day. Such a scale of destruction of rainforest was hard to contemplate. I felt inadequate in Sussex discussing the fate of our planet amongst friends and wanted to do something to help. The irony, of course, being that my travels made it clear to me that I needed to focus my work locally. And so I ended up at Prickly Nut Wood, just a couple of miles from the letterbox where the leaflets had arrived, the ones that sent me, young and headstrong, to the other side of the world. The story of *The Alchemist* by Paulo Coelho describes a similar realisation.

What my travels abroad showed me was a pattern. The pattern of the forest dweller. In the Amazon rainforest, and later in Papua New Guinea, I spent time with people who were children of generations of families who had dwelled within the forest. I met people to whom the forest was an extended map of provisions. They knew where to find medicinal plants to treat their ailments, they knew where migratory species would arrive and when, they lined their pathways with fruit-producing trees to eat from and harvest whilst on their journeys to visit friends or neighbours, and they built their houses from timber growing around them. These forests were rich in biodiversity, and the knowledge and lore of the forest had been passed on by its human inhabitants. Children grew up learning the different uses of plants, and where to find and harvest fruit-growing trees without realising they had learnt it. Education came through being brought up in one place, knowing that landscape, and being fully integrated into a way of life that was simple, although, of course, this life was not without its hardships. This tradition of the forest dweller being a natural form of woodland management seemed to be missing from the way forests were managed in England.

At Prickly Nut Wood, I wanted to live as a forest dweller, but I had not grown up as one and had no one to show me the lore of the land. I had to learn it through experience and observation, and I also had to transfer the pattern observed in diverse tropical rainforests to the woodlands of the south of England.

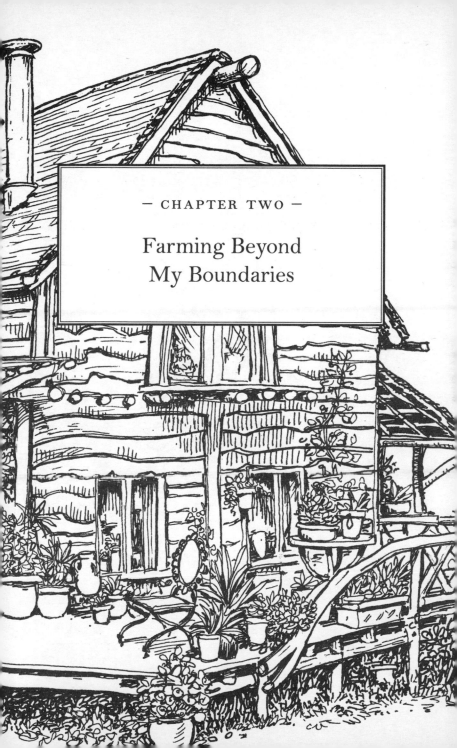

— CHAPTER TWO —

Farming Beyond
My Boundaries

During my year of observation, I expanded my knowledge of the locality by regularly walking the generous collection of footpaths that weave through the parish. In doing so, I began to build up a map of surrounding foraging sites to which I could seasonally return over the coming years.

If I strike east from Prickly Nut Wood, I pass through an ancient wooded common, which has not been grazed for many years. Large, outstretched, pollarded oaks cast dappled shade over what were once pastures, now patches of wood sedge and bracken. Dark pools surrounded by thickets of blackthorn make this enchanted woodland a fine source of sloes. Whether for wine or gin, these 'dry your mouth' plums are worth collecting as the flavour when fermented or steeped in a spirit brings laughter to most who partake in their pleasure. The blackthorn itself can be the most impenetrable of trees, with sharp thorns that tend to poison the skin when pricked. Many a time have I noticed what seemed a scratch from blackthorn inflame in to a septic wound. This tree deserves respect. I remember reading how a 14-foot-wide hedge of blackthorn was once planted around Farnham Castle for protection. In the days when a septic wound could be life-threatening, the use of blackthorn would have led any potential invaders to have second thoughts.

The common is bisected by the road and it is here my life nearly ended some years ago in a car crash. I mention this as I ended up in a hedge and a spike of blackthorn pierced my eye. In protecting itself my eye formed a cataract and I had to have the lens replaced, so I am fortunate still to have good vision. I returned to the site a few months after the accident and cut myself a blackthorn stick from the broken bush near where I'd had my collision. It has made a good walking stick and is a good reminder to me of the fragility of all life. Blackthorn makes excellent walking sticks but it is a challenge to cut – a good pair of gauntlets is recommended. As part of my winter work involves laying hedges, I have some very heavy-duty leather hedging gloves that enable me to grasp the stem of blackthorn others might shy away from.

Hedge laying has begun to see a renaissance over the past 20 years. Stewardship grants have led farmers and landowners to consider the wisdom of starting their tractors and spending the day 'flail cutting' the top and sides of the hedge, and using much diesel to destroy the biomass that has grown within the hedgerow. Laying a hedge involves 'pleaching' (partially cutting through) the upright stem, in order to bend the stem over and lay it at an angle so that it forms a woven barrier and all knits together. The top (in the style of the hedge laying I carry out) is woven with hazel binders around upright posts of sweet chestnut about 1 foot apart. The resulting hedge not only looks attractive and uniform but forms a strong, long-lasting and stock-proof barrier, removing the need to use steel fencing altogether. It can then be left to grow on for about fifteen years and the next time it is laid, there will be a firewood crop yielded from the hedge row as well as some interesting elbow shaped pieces of timber formed from the re-growth from the pleached stems. These pieces can make fine walking sticks or, as I have found, can be used to make traditional knees in boat building. My first rowing boat contains ash and chestnut knees formed from material sourced whilst hedge laying. Laying a hedge also creates the perfect nest-building habitat.

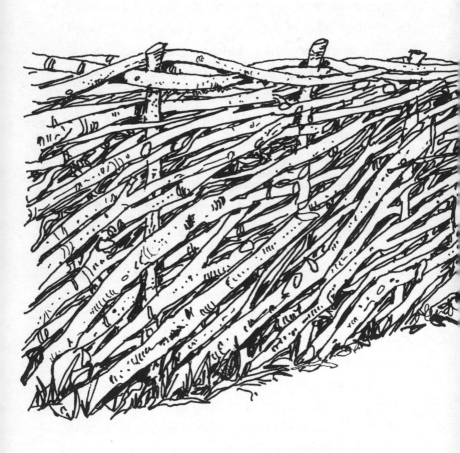

The angled stems, woven together and then supported by stakes and upright re-growth, make the ideal support for nest building. So a well-laid hedge will increase biodiversity, work as a stock fence, provide material for walking sticks and other projects, provide firewood, remove the need to use steel fencing, and can also provide a good site for foraging if the species used are well chosen. Surely this productive and diverse hedgerow, which can be managed with hand tools, must be a more sustainable alternative to repeated cutting with a tractor and flail cutter.

In 1992, I planted about a mile of hedging on a nearby property.

28 December

I was greeted this morning by the perfect winter day. A good, crisp frost meant I needed a couple of layers under my Swandri, but after an hour of work the sun was warming me and I shed a layer. I started on the hedgerow down the northern side of Meera's wood. This hedge will wind for about a mile and I look forward to the day when I can stand back and see the hedge in its full glory, matured and bursting with wildlife and wild food. It's hard to find words to encompass the sense of satisfaction and fulfilment I get

*from planting trees and hedgerows. Such work should
be part of everyone's life. A year of 'national service'
to improve our environment would be a good
statement for an evolving society.*

I chose hawthorn and blackthorn as the main species,
as they lay well and form an impenetrable boundary.
They also produce sloes and haws from which to
make wines or jellies. In addition, I planted hazel
to provide nuts and materials for craft use; spindle to
add diversity and create sticks for artists' charcoal;
field maple to have its sap tapped for wine; holly for
berries for the Christmas market; Guelder rose for
its medicinal cramp bark; dog rose and rugosa rose
for the hips for rose hip syrup; cherries for fruit (for
the birds); a few oak standards to grow and mature
from within the hedge to form ancient trees for
future generations, increasing the hedge's biodiversity; and crab apple for pollination and the making of
verjuice.

Verjuice

*Collect ripe crab apples and leave them in a plastic bag
to sweat. After a few days press out the juice and then
bottle it, leaving cotton wool in the top as it will*

*ferment because of the natural yeasts. It will be ready
in about a month and makes a traditional substitute
for lemon juice. It is particularly good in salad
dressings and stir fries.*

After eight good years of growth, I laid the hedge
and now sheep graze in the fields without any fencing, the hedge successfully keeping them within the
field. Planting hedgerows and laying hedges that I
can return to as I walk the parish, harvesting wild

food and produce that I know is there, form part of my farming of the surrounding countryside.

The common also has a good amount of self-seeded ash and this, entwined with honeysuckle, makes some of the most attractive 'barley twist' sticks I have ever made. In my early years at Prickly Nut Wood I sold walking sticks in the village pub. They sold well and it made a good talking point, helping me meet many people and further integrate into village life.

Bordering the common is one of the orchards I have planted over the past 20 years. Now the trees are producing well and the orchard provides cider apples for the village pressing. I planted 'Harry Masters Jersey', 'Crimson King', 'Yarlington Mill' and 'Kingston Black', and they all make a fine cider, whether mixed or fermented out to single-variety ciders. The trees are pruned as standards, which allows sheep to graze beneath, a traditional silvi-pastoral system that I expect we will see more of in the coming years. Lodsworth has always been a cider-making area and throughout the village well-established old trees can be seen, now enclosed in gardens from parts of the old orchards of days gone by. I remember old Ted Holmes telling me before he died of the mobile press that used to turn up outside

the Hollist Arms pub, and the excitement he experienced as a young lad on apple-pressing day.

Within the village we have revived the tradition, and each year we set up the press and 'masarators' outside the Hollist Arms. People bring apples and take away apple juice, and the remainder goes into barrels. This is fermented over the winter months in households throughout the village. The resulting cider is brought out for village celebrations, such as the village fête, or an anniversary or public holiday. Apple-pressing day is increasingly popular, with all ages mucking in and getting involved. At the end of the day the pulp from the apples is taken off to be fed to pigs, which in turn will taste fine with a glass of Lodsworth cider.

I remember the tasting on the first night we revived the tradition. It was election night when we brought the cider to the bar of the Hollist Arms. Nick Kennard was the landlord then, and with his wife Sally they ran the house well (although the beer was sometimes interesting!). The cider was strong that year and I noticed after a couple of hours that tongues were loosening, quite literally in the case of a respectable couple who worked for the European Union. The evening evolved into a party and the next morning Lodsworth was one place in England where many of the residents had no idea that Tony Blair had been elected for his first term as prime minister. Since that time our cider making has improved and the quality of the drink is more refined. Many a good winter's evening has been spent racking and blending to ensure the best quality is available for village functions.

*   *   *

Ted Holmes was a forester/coppice worker who worked mainly on the adjacent Cowdray estate. Ted would nod at me but rarely spoke – I was a different type of coppice worker, I lived up in the woods. One evening in the Hollist Arms, I bought Ted a beer or two, and he told me the story of his life as a boy in the village and the work he would do. His descriptions of village life painted a vivid picture for me – I could see his early-morning work in the bakery, then, moving on to the wheelwrights, how he would throw water over the metal tyre to cool it before it burned the wood of the wheel. Traditionally the metal tyre would be heated so that it expanded, and when it was glowing red it would be fitted over the wooden wheel rim and hammered into place. Once in place it was doused with water to stop burning the wood and the cooling process would shrink the metal tyre tight on to the wooden wheel, compressing it all together. A wheelwright was an important profession and with three blacksmiths all working in the village it was a thriving small community.

Ted talked to me about the cider, and in particular the plum and gage orchards that grew to the north of the village and the abundance of cob nuts along the eastern edge. Fruit picking formed part of his day as a boy as it does mine now. I've planted plums and gages in similar areas of the parish to where Ted mentioned they grew, and so far the trees have grown well and crops have been good. There is a lot of knowledge of our localities locked up in the memories of the older generations that will be useful in the future, when we are likely to need to become more locally based and self-supporting, and need to be able to turn our hands to a variety of different skills.

The cob nut orchard that ran along the eastern edge of the village has been lost amongst the many houses and gardens that have been built. Some gardens have one or two established nut trees remaining, but in a couple of places the orchard has remained intact and I've been fortunate to spend time restoring these areas.

When I first cut the derelict orchard, or 'platt', as a cob nut orchard is often called, it was a matter of cutting back thick, overgrown stems and reshaping the cob nut trees to form a goblet shape. The re-growth is then 'brutted' (snapped so that the branch is stressed and left to hang, still well attached to the mother tree by the fibres that are so strong in hazel wood). These goblet-shaped trees then produce an abundance of nuts. Commercially, most cob nut orchards are grown well away from woodland, in areas where squirrels are less likely to risk crossing open pasture to reach the delicious nuts dangling from the 'brutted' trees. I have now pruned the cob nut orchard on a couple of occasions and the trees are producing well once again.

Restoration of old fruit trees has kept me busy over many years and, by working in many individual gardens on the old trees, I've been able to see the patterns of the orchards that were once so much a part of our village landscape. Identifying old varieties is not easy; some are clearly distinctive but as many varieties have a similar 'parent' apple, identification can become difficult. One or two of the local Sussex varieties are easier to identify. 'Sussex Forge', an old cottagers' apple, dates from 1923. It is a small, yellow apple, streaked red with a red flush and is a good dual-purpose apple, as it cooks well and is of good flavour eaten fresh. The more I have worked with apples, the more respect and fascination I have for these wonderful fruits and the regional history that so many varieties bring with them. Our wild crab apple, *Malus sylvestris*, can often be found amongst ancient woodlands and was no doubt an important food and fermentation source for generations past, as were so-called 'wilding apples' (grown from discarded apples or cores) and cultivated varieties, the earliest of which recorded is the 'Pearmain'. This was the first named variety recorded and is noted on a deed of 1204. Since that time we have bred and crossbred apples to have a vast variety of cookers, eaters, dual-purpose, sliders, girlies and keepers – in fact the National Apple Collection in Brogdale, Kent, lists over one thousand varieties.

Planting new orchards is a favourite activity of mine. One must select a succession of varieties that will produce over a period of time, yet be part of the right overlapping pollination groups to ensure bees and other insects carry out their gift of duty. Some apples are tetraploids as opposed to diploids, so they need two other varieties to pollinate them. 'Blenheim Orange' and 'Bramley' seedlings are two well-known tetraploids. Most apples are then grafted onto a root stock, which dictates the height and expected lifespan of each tree. Most apple root stocks now used are root stocks that were developed at East Malling Research Station and hence have the name M from Malling, followed by a number. M25, for example, forms a large tree, whereas M27 forms a tiny tree. Which all makes it quite difficult when I'm asked that common question: 'I've got an old apple tree. Can you tell me what variety it is?'

Most small apple trees in gardens are on M26 rootstocks. These provide a relatively short-lived tree that will grow to about 10 feet (3m) in height and produce fruit at a young age. At Prickly Nut Wood I have a few apples on M26 rootstocks near the house and around the vegetable garden. Further afield I grow apples on the medium-sized MM106, and my largest apple trees are grafted on to M25. There are similar rootstocks for pears and plums. Most of my pears are on Quince A rootstock, which produces a large tree, with a few on Quince C, which produces a smaller, productive tree. Most of my plums are on the semi-vigorous rootstock St Julien, with a few near the house on the dwarfing rootstock Pixy, and a few larger plums on the vigorous Myrobalan B rootstock. Choosing the appropriate rootstock for the right situation – and visualising the heights and varieties – make planning and planting an orchard one of my favourite seasonal countryside activities. I am often

asked for advice on what to do with one field or another by a local landowner. In most cases I advise planting orchards. By planting standard trees (or planting maiden trees and pruning them to become standards) on large, vigorous root stocks well spaced out across the field, the orchard will establish well, allowing for grazing by sheep or geese below. These orchards are a beautiful landscape feature in their own right, brightening the fields every spring with blossom, the promise of fruit to come. The planting and establishment of orchards throughout the countryside will leave an important food legacy for the next generation.

Some of the most interesting work I did with apples was when I was working for Oxfam as a permaculture consultant in Albania. The mountain district I was working in was poor and inaccessible, and the choice of fresh fruits was very limited outside of the main growing season. The apples in particular were very poor. The local varieties were at best similar to low-quality English crab apples, so any improvement in the varieties grown would be beneficial to the local people. Working with Brogdale, suitable scion (grafting) material was obtained and sent out to Albania for grafting on to the local Albanian crab root stocks. 'Ribston Pippin' was chosen for its high level of vitamin C, while others were chosen to survive the long, cold winters and the short summer growing season in the mountains. These materials are now cultivated in the permaculture research centre in northern Albania, and hopefully improving the lives and diet of many people living a sustainable lifestyle in the mountains.

Restoring old fruit trees and orchards, as well as planting new ones, have helped me to cultivate many plants in the surrounding landscape, although I can't exactly claim that I am farming them.

As I turn and head south, with the sensual curves of the South Downs silhouetted in the distance, I join the small, winding waterway – the River Lod. Rising north-east of Lynchmere, and picking up many streams along its journey, it skirts the village of Lodsworth before joining the River Rother at Lod's Bridge, which in turn joins the Arun and continues on out to sea at Littlehampton. As the Lod winds south through the parish it makes its way through mixed coppice woodland – hazel, ash, field maple and willow – below which can be found abundant blue-bells, yellow archangel, early purple-flowering orchid and wood anemone in late spring. Preceding this flush of colour, the wood is carpeted with the dense mass of foliage of wild garlic. A walk this way in spring and you will be aware of the wild garlic before you see it. Its poignant aroma fills the air well in advance of its physical presence. I harvest the wild garlic for stir-fries and salads, a cheese sandwich for lunch is greatly enhanced by a few leaves, and it makes an excellent pesto. I have supplied pubs and restaurants with the leaves over the years, and in my early days at Prickly Nut Wood I would often trade beer for wild garlic at the local hostelries.

The Lod is a healthy, clean river and salmon trout spawn as far up as the mill pond at Lurgashall. Brown trout are common, as are bream, roach, chub and pike. As a small river it is not often fished, with the nearby River Rother being more popular with anglers. One part of the river that seems never short of water is near the bridge at Lickfold. The road regularly floods here, and after heavy rains it can be hard to make out what is bridge and what is river. There have been a number of civil engineering works over the past couple of years to try to improve the regular flooding, but so far I have seen little evidence that they have made much difference. I am astonished at how often we seem to throw money at trying to find a solution to a problem that is part of nature. Water has clearly always flooded at Lickfold, which is a low point for water collection and is well fed from surrounding fields. It is not a major route, is only impassable for a few days a year and there are alternative routes, so it would seem to make sense to leave the river to flood when it wishes at Lickfold Bridge and focus our civil engineering energies on more useful projects.

Where the Lod reaches halfway bridge, I have found many good giant puffballs in the adjacent fields. Creating a fungi map based on wild mushrooms that I find is a useful part of farming the surrounding landscape, and there are many areas that I visit purely to collect mushrooms for the table. One of my favourite is 'horn of plenty', or the 'black trumpet'. I have a favourite picking spot heading west from Prickly Nut Wood. When found in abundance I have picked baskets full, and as I often find them near to Halloween, they are an ideal mushroom to market to local restaurants for 'black trumpet soup'. Another favourite I find throughout the chestnut coppice is 'chicken of the woods'. This is a great find, as one orange bracket of 'chicken of the woods' can feed a good number of people. I've walked through the woods to the Duke of Cumberland pub at Henley, and found and traded 'chicken of the woods' for beer on a few occasions. 'Chicken of the woods' gets its name mainly from its consistency; follow a recipe for chicken pie, substitute 'chicken of the woods' for real chicken, and few people will notice the difference. When cooked, 'chicken of the woods' looks exactly like chicken, and its texture and taste are surprisingly similar.

As a lover of mushrooms, I have taken to cultivating my own. I have been growing mushrooms on logs for about 12 years now and have had good success with Japanese shiitake mushrooms and oyster mushrooms. I buy in the mushroom spawn growing on sawdust and then drill holes out in a log, fill them with the sawdust spawn and seal them with hot wax.

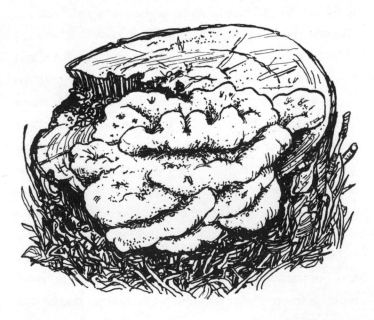

In my first year of inoculating (as this process is called), I used beeswax from my hives and the bees visited the logs and took back every bit of the wax. Since then I have used a vegetable-based cheese wax, similar to what you will find surrounding Edam cheese.

The log is left to stand within the woodland for a year to 18 months, depending on the species of tree. A birch log, for instance, will produce mushrooms more quickly than a sweet chestnut log, because the mycelium can colonise birch more easily as it's less durable than chestnut. Once the mycelium has spread through the log, the log will fruit (produce mushrooms naturally) when the appropriate weather conditions arrive. In autumn, with heavy rains following the warmth of summer, the conditions are perfect to stimulate mushrooms to appear in great numbers throughout the countryside. The same applies with mushrooms cultivated on logs. One great advantage of inoculating logs is that I know each log contains mushrooms and therefore I can simulate the autumn rains by throwing the logs into my pond. I leave them there for 48 hours and then extract them. About five days later the mushrooms will start appearing. The log should be rested for about six weeks before shocking it again. This process can be repeated so each log can produce mushrooms three to four times a year. I think of the process of shocking the log into fruiting as being that the mycelium inside the log feels like it is drowning as it lies in the pond partially submerged. When nature is under stress it reproduces, so naturally the mycelium sends out its reproductive parts, these being the edible mushrooms.

16 April

I took my 'push me/pull me' hedge-laying tool, which resembles an exaggerated boat hook, down to the pond. I pulled out another five sweet chestnut logs and stacked them in the shade nearby. The logs I pulled out four days ago already have tiny mushrooms beginning to form. I am going to keep up this pattern of shocking a few more every two days and see what volumes I produce. I enjoy walking amongst my log piles. To a visitor they would look like any other pile of firewood, but I know there are mushrooms stored in the log, waiting for me to free them. Today, with so many piled up at different stages, I felt like I was wandering through an outdoor laboratory, inspecting different stages of an experiment. Took 2 kg to the Hollist Arms – Sam is going to stuff them with walnuts and Stilton, and serve them as a starter.

I often think that, as a species, the human race is under high levels of stress. Our reaction to this stress, similar to the mushrooms, is to reproduce, and in doing so we maintain the seemingly unstoppable upward curve of our increasing population. I once heard on the radio that had China not adopted its one-child policy, over the past 25 years their population would have increased by the size of the population of Europe (and that's not counting all the children who were born). With our rapidly growing population, and the associated challenges of meeting our energy and food needs, it is possible with hindsight to see the wisdom in what at first glance seems such a Draconian measure. It probably seems a step too far for Western cultures to consider such a measure. But sooner rather than later we are going to have to make some major decisions about population control – unless nature, through natural disasters or contagious diseases, decides to make them for us. I find this one of the most difficult environmental questions of all – and as a father of three children, I understand the animalistic need and drive to procreate. In the United Kingdom as a whole, and especially in the south-east of England, we are very heavily populated. It is hard to see how we can maintain population growth at its present rate, whilst at the same time converting more potentially food-producing land into accommodation and harvesting more resources for energy and infrastructure, without further degrading our landscape and pushing more species towards extinction. However, despite this rather negative outlook, it is important to remember that a new generation always brings fresh hope. Perhaps it is the children of the next generation who will make these tough decisions about population growth, limit our energy usage rather than expand it, develop local food and energy initiatives to revitalise communities,

and simplify our lives to bring us more in touch with nature and our natural environment.

*   *   *

Foraging has become a natural part of any walk I take and I am always alert to a free meal that nature is offering. Crossing some of the many rural roads near Prickly Nut Wood, one becomes aware of one of the few benefits of the motor car to the forager. Motor cars are quite adept at producing a meal and I've collected a good number of pheasants and rabbits, one partridge, one mallard duck and a number of roe deer, all of which have provided fine meals. The quality of roadkill varies depending upon the nature of the vehicle's impact and where it has struck the animal. Whilst I have picked up pheasants so crushed and flattened that it would not have been worth trying to sort the meat from the bone, I have found others where the impact has been slight and the meat is untarnished. The next thing to establish is how long the animal has been dead. First check for warmth and how flexible the body is – has rigor mortis set in? Then look for flies' eggs, which can arrive within an hour in the heat of summer. Have any hatched in to maggots? Does the meat smell? If I decide it is good to eat, I still have to get the meat back home. This is easy with a rabbit or a pheasant, but not so easy with a roe deer. If it is a deer I find, the first thing I look for is to see whether the stomach has begun to swell. Deer are ruminants and the grass in their stomachs will ferment, making the stomach inflate with gas. If the stomach is not swollen I will 'paunch' the deer – cut open its belly, and remove the stomach and intestines. If the deer is still warm, at this stage I will remove the liver and take it back home for my next meal. I will then drag the deer into the shade, marking the spot clearly in my mind so I can return to it later with a vehicle and collect the carcass. Once I have the carcass back home, I hang it in a fly-free environment for a few days before skinning and butchering it. A roadkill deer will provide venison for a number of meals, and such a find often signals a good time to invite over friends for a fine casserole or roast. The actual killing of deer is controlled under the Deer Act, so don't let the delicious taste of venison tempt you into hunting deer, unless you decide to get properly trained through a deer-stalking course with the associated firearms certificates.

Heading north on the return journey to Prickly Nut Wood, the footpath takes me under an old walnut tree that kindly deposits large volumes of nuts upon the footpath. The actual walnut we are all familiar with is enclosed within an outer case that is thick and green. The green colouring will soon stain your fingers when harvesting these nuts. It has been traditionally used as a dye, as have the leaves. After picking a bagful of nuts and husks and then trying to wash your hands of the greeny/brown colouring, you will certainly appreciate its qualities for dyeing. I have five mature walnut trees I visit for foraging nuts as I walk around the parish, and there are a couple I have planted at Prickly Nut Wood. I planted grafted varieties of 'Broadview' and 'Buccaneer', which have struggled to compete with the ever-present challenge of the grey squirrel. I visited Martin Crawford's nut trials at the agro-forestry research trust in South Devon and saw some fine examples of grafted walnuts producing well, which are all very suitable for our climate here. Martin recommended the variety 'Fernette' in particular, but there are a number of good cultivars to choose from. Away from the woods, where squirrels have less aerial access to trees, the planting of more walnuts would be a useful addition to our future food supply. In any garden or wasteland space, the planting of fruit- or nut-producing trees will help us towards having more established perennial food production, something that I believe will become a necessity in the future.

As I continue north beyond Prickly Nut Wood, I take a favourite route that takes me up the zigzag to Blackdown. On the way through Blackdown Park, I pass an orchard of plums and apples that I planted ten years earlier. The trees are now well established and cropping well, and sheep graze beneath them – a classic silvi-pastoral landscape. The zigzag is a steep climb up to the Temple of the Winds, where a stone bench marks one of the finest views in the south of England. Looking out from the Temple of the Winds, it is hard to imagine the motor car has been invented or that we are anywhere near the highly populated south of England. The border between Sussex and Surrey passes over Blackdown, and the area was one of the first pieces of land the National Trust acquired. In recent times – with the felling of timber and the grazing of cattle – much of the hillside has been returned to heathland.

I often visit here with my children for bilberry picking, as the reduction in tree cover has encouraged the spread of this prolific berry across the open heath. The wild relative of the blueberry, it is delicious in flavour and ensures the children's hands and faces are more purple than when we have been blackberrying. Plenty are consumed while picking but others are taken home for one of my seasonal favourites –

bilberry pancakes. I remember as a child that straw-berries had a particular season. Now, with imported food, it is possible to eat them all year round, and the energy cost of transporting them is reflected in the price, unlike the associated pollution. The excitement and anticipation of waiting for the first strawberries to ripen have been taken away and in doing so this exquisite fruit – at its best when plucked straight from the plant – has become trapped in a plastic pack-age and transported around the globe. It is the eating of fruit in their particular season that makes our connection with growing food so special and forag-ing such a delight. Blueberries are readily available all year round, but bilberries, they have their season and even then you will not find them in the shops. This perfect little berry creates a day of adventure. A picnic is prepared, water bottles filled and a mission undertaken to venture out across the heathland. A whole day unveils itself around this seasonal fruit. Games of hide and seek are interspersed with more picking. My son Zed becomes a bilberry scout, venturing ahead and alerting us busy pickers behind him to the treasures he discovers. Tess, my daughter, is picking well, her face blotched purple from her stained fingers. 'Look at this one,' she shrieks, finding a good-sized bilberry. As the day draws on she is on my shoulders as we start our descent and the journey home.

Foraging engages you with the countryside and all it has to offer. It is an experience that will etch itself on your memory, a world away from purchasing a punnet of blueberries at a supermarket. Added to that, it is a healthy day out that costs nothing – and you often end up with a free lunch!

I can't finish writing about foraging without mentioning the sweet chestnut. One of the main foraging activities at Prickly Nut Wood takes place during the chestnut season. Although I should properly refer to it as harvesting rather than foraging, as the trees surrounding my home produce large amounts and collecting them is quick and rewarding. The sweet chestnut (*Castanea sativa*) was introduced by the Romans for its delicious and nutritious nuts, and is now so well established in the woodland landscape that it is often referred to as an 'honorary native'. In my early days at Prickly Nut Wood, I harvested sacks of the nuts and sold some to Steve Jones, a fine independent greengrocer at Fernhurst, whilst others I bartered for beer in some of the local pubs. Chestnuts are well adapted to cope with the awaiting grey squirrels. Unlike hazelnuts, chestnuts have a spiky case and the squirrels have to wait until the chestnut case opens before they are able to harvest the nut. The case opens to produce three nuts, which most years ripen to a reasonable size. The grey squirrel has its opportunity but so do I, and there are always plenty of nuts to go round. The best method for harvesting I've found is to throw a tarpaulin under the tree. The nuts fall on to the tarpaulin and are easy to sort from their cases, and the remains are swept away. A few hours later I can return, knowing all the nuts on the tarpaulin are freshly fallen. Picking

this way, I ensure quality nuts and do not waste time picking amongst the piles of all the cases that build up under a productive chestnut tree.

I have eaten chestnuts in numerous ways, from bread and biscuits to nut roasts, soups and chutneys, but I still find it hard to beat roasting them on the open fire. I have a French chestnut-roasting pan I was given, like a frying pan with a woven metallic base. Although a functional object, it is beautifully designed and is always a pleasure to put into use. I take autumn walks through the coppice and return with pockets full of chestnuts, then sit around the outdoor kitchen fire roasting chestnuts and looking out across the woodland – so many times with so many different people, the experiences all meld into one, one taste-provoking, magical experience that encapsulates autumn at Prickly Nut Wood.

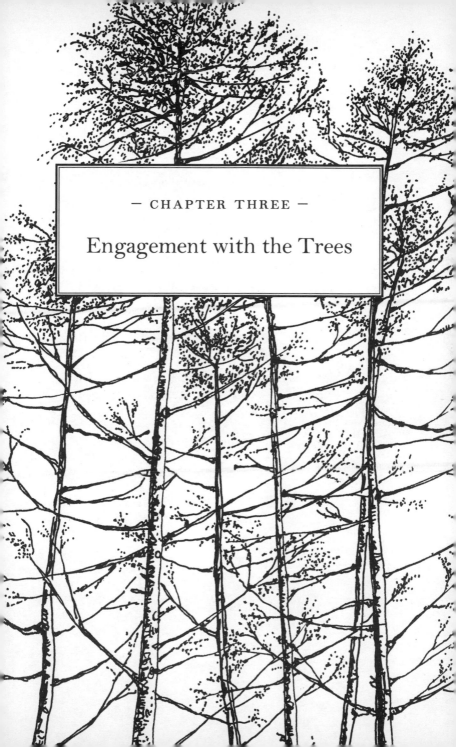

— CHAPTER THREE —

Engagement with the Trees

As my year of observation began to reach its end I started to consider my plans for the management of the woodland. Observation had been a privilege, and with that focused time I had learned so much more detail than the hustle and bustle of life generally allows us. Now I was engaging with the prospect of reworking some of the derelict coppices and introducing some of my own ideas, such as the planting of coppice fruit avenues.

Coppice fruit avenues are where fruit trees are intentionally planted between cants of coppice, or in clearings next to cants. When a cant is cut, sunlight reaches the fruit trees, causing the formation of fruit buds and the promise of a good crop the following year.

I clearly remember cutting my first cant of coppice. It had last been cut some 50 years earlier and had some larger-diameter stems, as well as areas of wind-blow and deadwood. There is a sense of history within the woods that feels like a tangible link when you cut coppice.

Coppice is the term used to describe the successional cutting of broadleaf woodland during the dormant winter period. In spring, when the sap rises, the stump of the tree (known in coppicing as the 'stool') sends up new shoots that are grown on for a number of years until they reach the desired size. They are then cut again during winter and the process is repeated over again. The wood cut from coppice is known as 'underwood', and has for centuries catered for a variety of traditional products and supported a large rural workforce, from the cutter and coppice merchant to the craftsman. Coppice is a valuable crop and, managed well, can sustain more people in work per acre than any other modern forestry alternative. It is also a sustainable pattern of management: trees rarely need replanting, so the soil is not disturbed and therefore not subject to the risk of erosion. Nutrients are returned to the soil mainly through annual leaf fall. Coppicing creates a cyclical habitat and unique ecosystem, and is one of the few patterns of symbiosis known in nature in which human beings form a crucial part of the relationship.

In a well-managed coppice, the stools are closely spaced about five foot apart, and the ground is fully shaded by the leaves and coppice shoots. When the poles are cut, sunlight pours in, dormant seeds waiting for the light sprout, and different birds, animals and insects move into the newly created habitat.

I feel in touch with the woodsmen of old when I sit down around the brash fire and contemplate the previous cut, and the one before that. Coppice woods carry history within them, and with it they carry hope for the future. A truly sustainable landscape is one where the sustainable practices of previous generations are being repeated in the present in order to leave resources and opportunities for the future. Coppicing is one of the few landscapes in which humans are an integrated part of the ecosystem and where taking resources from the landscape produces positive by-products. Each area that has been coppiced allows in the sunlight that helps wildflowers thrive, which in turn provide food to caterpillars and fills the woods with summer butterflies. If we remove the human element, the woods return to high forest, the varied patchwork disappears, the wildflowers recede with the shade, and there is no food for the caterpillars and butterflies. This remarkable ecosystem is dependent on the coppice worker, cutting his

or her annual quota of poles from which to make a living. In Bradfield Woods in Suffolk, managed by the Suffolk Wildlife Trust, coppicing was practised before 1252, according to Oliver Rackham in his seminal work *Ancient Woodland*. These woods contain some 370 species of plants, and this vastly diverse woodland has developed over the past thousand years by humans cutting poles on a cyclical basis for their needs. In return, nature has responded by creating a unique patchwork of plants in the shadow of our small-scale timber-harvesting operations.

Nature is constantly trying to create woodland. As human beings, we control nature in different phases of this evolution and in the example of coppicing, we create a diverse woodland that we keep on a rotational cycle of perhaps seven years, in the case of hazel. If we take a field that we don't cut or graze with livestock, the grass will become long and tufty, and then perennial plants such as brambles will appear. Next come the pioneer tree species such as birch and willow. These colonise the area quickly but will only form a temporary canopy, and over time the climax canopy species, such as oak, beech or ash, will find their way to the top and become the canopy layer. This is what we refer to as 'nature's climax'. This is the point where the evolution from earth to high forest has reached its final point; beyond this climax layer nature does not evolve further but rather waits for a canopy tree to fall over and, when the light is let back in down to the forest floor, the process begins once more.

With coppicing we have kept nature to within a certain point of that cycle. By regularly restricting the re-growth of, for instance, hazel, to seven years, nature is not allowed to reach its climax.

The wonderfully diverse flora of chalk grassland has been established through keeping nature at close to ground level. Grazing with sheep ensures that the pioneer tree species do not become established and begin the upward journey to becoming woodland. When we look at landscapes rich in biodiversity, coppice woodlands and chalk grassland are two very different landscapes. The first came about because of the need for small-diameter poles, the second because of the need for wool and meat. These land-use patterns that produce food and materials for our needs whilst maintaining a rich, biodiverse landscape should be the models we use to help us design future landscape strategies.

I spent a good while when surveying my first cant of coppice not just looking at the timber, the direction of felling, the dead wood and hung-up branches, but also searching for the best extraction routes for the timber. As mentioned, the soils of Wealden clay in the wood are on the north-east face of the hill and are impassable with a vehicle most winters. Extraction needs to be by hand, by horse, or winched from a hard ride to the woodland edge. Some of the 40-year-old coppice poles were up to 14 inches in diameter at the base and immovable without some sort of mechanical aid. I have experimented with most forms of extraction over the years and the key is choosing the right equipment for the right wood. With coppice woodlands, where much of the cut material can be turned into product, it is often sensible to do the conversion within the wood. Large poles can be cleaved into four pieces for posts and rail fencing, which is the vernacular fencing style throughout Sussex. When making pales for chestnut-paling fence, I've built a cleaving break in the middle of the cant. The timber is processed in the wood and tied up into bundles of 25 pieces, easy to carry out on the shoulder, while the bark and any off-cuts are left in the wood itself. Hurdle makers will often set up and make hurdles in the coppice. Cutting enough material to work up and make hurdles from takes a couple of days. This way, as they work through the woods, they are carrying out only the finished hurdle. When we cut five-year-rotation chestnut coppice for yurt poles and bean poles, we work it up with a bill hook and carry it out the woods on our shoulders. Each journey out of the woods without carrying a bundle is a wasted extraction journey.

The use of horses is making a steady recovery in English woodlands. Although some are being used in agriculture and horticulture, it is in the forest that horses can be uniquely valuable. Coming in a range of sizes, all with different pulling powers, selecting the right breed for the right woodland is vital. In coppice woods, from which lighter poles are extracted, a cob can do plenty of the work and cause minimal damage to the ground flora. When larger timbers need moving it seems hard to better an Ardenne, which are stocky horses with immense power. A number of years ago I engaged Richard Branscombe and the Working Horse Trust, with their reliable Ardennes Monty and Dylan, to extract about 80 oak trees for a barn we were building.

17 May

It's day two of the extraction and I arrived to find Monty and Dylan tethered to the horsebox, feeding up on some hay. I think yesterday was hard work for these two horses. They spend a lot of time pulling carts, but this is real work and they knew it. All harnessed up, we walk back along the ride and hitch Monty up to the forwarder. I'm impressed with the voice commands – the control Richard has is firm but calm. Monty pulled up alongside an oak butt, this one about 15 foot long and 20 inches in diameter. After yesterday's sharp learning curve for all of us, today it seems more instinctual as we prepare the forwarder and lay log bearers for the log to roll up, while Richard attaches Monty to pull and roll the log up the bearers on to the forwarder. It's impressive to see the tension in Monty's muscles as he pulls forward and in doing so safely negotiates getting the log to stop, centrally positioned on the forwarder. Monty is then hitched up again to the front of the forwarder and commences his return journey back through the woods. He stops perfectly, aligning the log and forwarder with the sawmill. This pattern – but with changing the horses – continues throughout the day. As the afternoon draws on, we approach a large butt that looks far too heavy, even to the hard-working Monty and Dylan. Richard decides they will pull the forwarder together. All hitched up, but no number of commands would make them budge. Richard instructs me to take Dylan's bridle and run with him, and he'll do the same with

Monty. Sure enough, the horses picked up the pace and our encouragement was enough to start the forwarder moving. I felt truly alive running next to Dylan and encouraging him all the way. When we arrived back at the sawmill, it was the end of the day. Time to feed and rest the horses. We all had a smile on our faces. It doesn't make me feel like that when I extract with a tractor.

I've extracted with ropes and pulleys, using a vehicle stationed on a hard ride (stone track) to drive forwards and in doing so pull the timber to the edge of the ride. This is an effective system but reduces the life of your clutch! A better alternative is a forestry winch, which is powered and driven from a tractor's three-point linkage. Many are remote-controlled, and the one I use works off two cords. I can stand well away from the operating area and pull one cord to start the winch and the other to stop it. The winch pulls the timber to the back of the tractor, where it is secured with a logging chain. It is then possible to winch more trees – my little 50 hp tractor will take three or four small butts at a time.

Only in cold winters when the ground freezes solid is it possible to drive into the woods and collect poles with a pick-up truck. This doesn't happen every winter, and so when it does it is important to make the most of it. On icy mornings when the ground is hard I will extract until the sun comes up and starts to warm the surface of the woodland soil. Being on the north side of the hill, my hours of winter sun are limited and this is one of the few times it seems an advantage.

Back in the coppice, I am beginning to fell some of the smaller poles and deadwood. The deadwood is extracted for firewood – it will already be well seasoned and dry, but I do not take all of it. Some standing deadwood should always be left as it is an important part of woodland biodiversity. A coppiced wood with a few upright, dead stems can look strange to the uninitiated, but when you stand at the edge of the wood in early spring and listen to the resonance of a drumming woodpecker, the value of those standing dead stems becomes more obvious.

The smaller poles I lay in drifts to be worked up, which is standard practice in most coppice woodlands. By felling the poles in the same direction and then laying them in rows all facing the same way, I end up with a series of these drifts, looking like rivers of brash flowing through the coppice. I then start at the end of the drift and work up the poles from the butt to the tip. Because they are lying in drifts, it is possible to pick up the next pole with relative ease, whereas when they are not drifted the poles will snag and tangle as you try to separate them. I work up my poles with a Morris's Devon bill hook, my preferred pattern of bill hook to use for this job. Bill hooks (or handbills) are an ancient tool, and many different shapes and patterns were made for different regions and uses. It is possible to find a good second-hand bill hook that, with a few hours of dedicated sharpening, will return to its former glory and keep the new generation of coppicers in business for many a year. Makes to look out for are: Moss, Fussells, Elwell, Brades, Gilpin, Harrison … there are many others. As work on the land became mechanised the range of bill hooks declined, and most that are now readily available are inferior tools. These are often not made of tempered steel, and they therefore do not hold a good edge. One company still making traditional bill hooks at their hammer forge near Exeter is Morris's of Dunsford. They make about five patterns of bill hook, plus an excellent double-handed Yorkshire hedging bill hook. These hooks are properly tempered and are ideal for working coppice woodland. Finding a good bill hook is the first step; learning to sharpen it is the next.

For sharpening second-hand bill hooks – or a hook that has really lost its edge or has been misused so that there is a small dink in the metal – I turn to my 30-inch waterwheel. This sandstone wheel I picked up a number of years ago from Arthur Rudd's. Arthur runs a building and reclamation yard near Passfield. His yard is an Aladdin's cave and yet remarkably he seems to know where everything is! Arthur has a great knowledge of bricks that needs recording before he departs this world. But back to the grind-stone … it has an MOD symbol on the frame and was made in Falkirk in 1942. I have always imagined it was used for bayonet sharpening during the Second World War. It takes two people to sharpen the bill hook: one to turn the wheel with its crank handle, the other to press the bill hook against the stone at the appropriate angle as it turns.

Sharpening a bill hook involves first sharpening the shoulder of the blade, as the key to getting a clean cut with a bill hook is that there is a smooth transition between the edge of the hook and the shoulder of the blade. Having ground down the shoulder a little, I then move on to the edge. Although the grindstone wheel can create a reasonable edge, to create an edge for coppicing and working up I like to usc a Japanese ceramic stone. These water stones are first worked over the shoulder and then the edge, and their natural clay is worked away during the sharpening process, leaving a glistening edge. My Devon bill hook is lovely and sharp and works up the coppice

pole with minimum effort, removing all the side growth and small knots. I then slice off the tip of the pole with one swing of the bill hook. I always cut the poles at an angle as the hook will slice through the grain at an angle with ease.

Many days of winter pass and my pile of coppice poles grows. The small side shoots keep the kettle boiling on the small brash fire that keeps me company throughout the winter days in the woods. Many days are still, some wet and windy, and many are crisp, clear and bright. On these mornings in the magic of a Sussex woodland, there is nowhere better on this earth to spend your day.

17 January

Glorious morning – stepped out to be greeted by a hoar frost. The trees were glistening as if embroidered with miniature icicles, the landscape was still, silent and magical. As I reached the copse my fire site stood out as it alone was clear of frost. Faint, occasional wisps of smoke were enough to let me know there was life in the embers. I stirred the embers with a stick and they responded with a reassuring red glow. I added some more twigs, put the kettle on top and then began to work on my bill hook with a Japanese stone ...

With the smaller poles cut and sorted, it is time to fell the larger stems. Removing the smaller poles has created more space and made a safer working area. Felling the larger stems is also about not creating a tangle of poles, so it is important to thoroughly sned up each pole after felling, and think carefully about felling directions and extraction routes. There are a number of different felling cuts that are designed for trees growing straight, leaning forwards and leaning backwards. All of these are best learnt with proper instruction and one should not undertake any chain-saw felling work without having passed the appropriate felling modules.

Before beginning to fell the larger trees, I have already selected a chestnut to grow on as a standard, not for timber in this case but for nut production. A few carefully chosen standards, whose branches will stand above the coppice, will help produce good nut crops while the coppice is regenerating.

I cannot help but be annually amazed by the variety of re-growth from sweet chestnut coppice. This management system, which produces a yield of sustainable timber whilst increasing biodiversity and enabling livelihoods, is one of the best models of sustainability that *Homo sapiens* has created. Despite this amazing model, we still have thousands of acres of derelict coppice in the United Kingdom that would clearly benefit from management and re-coppicing. In order to provide materials for building and fuel to keep us warm, a sustainable yield of timber will need to form a large part of any future plans.

*　　*　　*

When I first wanted to get some experience of coppicing, getting access to woodlands to gain that experience was very difficult. Some colleges held coppicing modules, but from talking with students these were rarely for more than a couple of days of actual practical work. There were volunteer opportunities available with conservation groups and wildlife trusts where some experience could be gained, but to get one-to-one with an under-woodsman was highly unlikely. The lack of desire to share knowledge appeared to come from a generation whose craft was their livelihood; if they shared it with another, they seemed to feel threatened by the competition that a new generation might bring. I clearly remember visiting a hurdle maker on a few occasions who was always happy to stop and chat but would never pick up a tool in my company. I've heard many similar stories. Sadly, it seems there are some old woodsmen who would rather take their knowledge to the grave than pass it on.

Fortunately, much of this has now changed, and the woodsmen of the new generation are keen to share knowledge and see the next generation coming through. There are some good apprenticeship schemes available, and a few more woodsmen are beginning to take on trainees on a one-to-one basis. Networking groups, such as regional coppice groups, offer opportunities to meet like-minded people, and keep abreast of news and information within the industry.

I remember clearly the first-ever meeting of the Sussex and Surrey Coppice Group, which we held at the Hollist Arms in Lodsworth. To this day I am still uncertain as to how the news of the meeting travelled as widely as it did, but the evening was memorable, to say the least. I had helped Linda Glynn of the Wessex Coppice Group to organise the meeting, she had sent messages out and we were expecting between 10 to 15 people. Nick Kennard, the landlord of the Hollist Arms, had offered us the snug – a cosy room with a log fire, ideal for a woodsmen's meeting. However, it wasn't long before the snug was full and the bar was filling up, too. Quite literally, characters were coming out from the woods to see what it was all about. Nick offered us the restaurant, and with the pub packed with woodland folk we began the meeting. Not long after it commenced, a character who resembled Gandalf from *The Lord of the Rings* appeared, with a twisted, carved staff, a long, forked beard, and sparkling eyes that lay beneath his thatch of hair. Never again did we receive such a turnout at a meeting, and I've not come across many of those characters since. I can only presume that they melted back into the Sussex woods and carried on with life as usual.

I helped with the launch of the Hampshire Coppice Group and the Dorset Coppice Group, and believe that with a voice and a place to network, coppice woodlands and their workers stand a better chance of active management and viable livelihoods, as we approach challenging times ahead. Coppice woodlands may be our most sustainable woodland resource, but there are many other woodland types and management strategies in the woods surrounding Prickly Nut Wood.

There is an area of woodland to the north of Prickly Nut Wood that I look after. It is what is referred to in forestry terms as a 'PAWS' – a plantation on an ancient woodland site. There was a period during the early 1970s when it became popular to

plant-up ancient woodland with fast-growing coniferous species. The reason was purely financial. Many
broadleaved ancient woodlands were seen as low
value, and by planting a fast-growing coniferous
species an ancient woodland could provide a return
within the lifetime of the landowner. This was a
major departure from the way high forest had previ-
ously been managed in the UK. Timber plantations
have been grown over long rotations – oak is often
grown for 120 to 150 years before felling – so the
norm was that you would be planting trees for your
grandchildren and harvesting what your grandpar-
ents had planted for you. This process ensured a yield
of timber was sustained for at least the next two
generations. High forest management has always
worked in long rotations. Planting trees that you
know will supply timber for your grandchildren's
generation is a positive way of ensuring future generations have the necessary resources, although alternative silvicultural techniques, such as continuous
cover forestry, can also supply a sustainable yield of
timber for future generations whilst taking better
care of woodland soils and biodiversity.

Ancient woodlands often contain a unique mixture
of plant species that have established over hundreds
of years, living in conjunction with one another. The

planting of a fast-growing coniferous species can have a major impact on these delicate woodland systems, and the denser the shade created, the quicker the ground flora dies out through lack of light. The soils may contain dormant seed that can regenerate many of the plant species, but the sooner the shade is removed the better the chance of recovery. The planting of coniferous plantations on ancient woodland sites commenced for purely short-term economic reasons, and nature was sidelined for economic gain. I'm not against the planting of coniferous species but appropriate land, such as agricultural cereal land, would be far preferable. In addition, there are plenty of other options for improving the economic viability of ancient woodlands, which I hope will become clearer as you read on.

I remember my first visit to the PAWS I now look after. It was a spring morning and I was drawn to the mass of bluebells thick beneath its coniferous canopy; wood spurge and the sparkle of wood anemone completed the picture. What was fortunate with this PAWS was that the coniferous species was European larch (*Larix decidua*). Larch is a deciduous conifer and loses its needles in the autumn in a similar manner to the way a broad-leafed tree loses its leaves. This, of course, allows light in and enables the ancient woodland flora to continue to flourish. Over time the larch needles may over-acidify the soil, but that is unlikely in one cycle of larch planting. This is one situation where allowing the plantation to grow on into a valuable crop would seem to be the sensible option over the fast removal of all the trees in the plantation.

However, it is back to assessment and surveying before I can make such a decision. The ground flora needs a professional survey, and for that I was lucky enough to have the Sussex Botanical Society and its interest in woodlands. Such organisations are responsible for so many of our detailed records of our ground flora and, working as a group, they can cross-reference between themselves if there is any dispute over species. The information they record gives me a benchmark of the current diversity of ground flora. A further survey in 10 to 15 years time should help to judge whether my management strategies are helping to increase or decrease biodiversity.

Although plantation forestry – both coniferous and deciduous – has been the main commercial silvicultural system in the UK for a number of years, I have never felt comfortable with the end result being a clear fell. Clear felling a plantation can have dramatic effects for the wildlife and there is a notable risk of soil erosion on sloping hillsides. The water table naturally rises after a clear fell and what was once a mature woodland can often look like a battle zone.

Continuous cover forestry is a better alternative to clear fell plantation forestry. The principles behind continuous cover forestry involve keeping the canopy predominantly intact and only removing clumps of trees, thereby opening up the forest floor to the light in a similar manner that would occur if a tree or trees blew over or died in an unmanaged woodland. The light reaching the forest floor then allows for natural regeneration or planting to take place. This method of forestry avoids the risk of soil erosion but does incur the need for more precise felling to avoid damaging younger growing trees and can make extraction to a ride more difficult. However, by using horses or appropriate extraction equipment – and by bringing the sawmill to the log rather than taking the log to the sawmill – these potential problems can be overcome. Existing plantations can be converted to continuous cover forestry by selective felling and re-planting of small areas, and allowing a more mixed-species woodland to develop. A continuous cover forest should contain a range of different ages and species of trees, and over time should build up a diverse flora and fauna.

Much of my work at Prickly Nut Wood and the surrounding woodlands I manage has involved derelict coppice restoration. The importance of coppice woodlands has inspired me to get more derelict woodland restored so it is able to provide useful poles once again. Restoring derelict coppice can be a hard and laborious process, but standing back and overseeing the fresh new re-growth from a newly restored, once-derelict coppice gives a lot of job satisfaction to a woodsman.

5 January

Finished the last of the hazel today. And it feels like a moment of celebration, a breakthrough in what has been a challenge of disentangling awkward stems that have grown high into the canopy, searching for light. As we chopped the last of the hazel brash for the fire and sat down to enjoy lunch, we all knew we had reached a milestone. Even our lunch today was more elaborate than usual: baked potatoes with olive oil and tamari, and tender squirrels slow-cooked in the fire embers, wrapped in foil with a little olive oil, garlic and rosemary. A fine cooking method for younger squirrels. Our conversation moved onto felling the birch, ash and chestnut. Nick and Kris, having just

*gained their chainsaw certificates, seemed naturally
eager to get felling. The extra sawing will be most
welcome.*

We cut five acres of derelict coppice that winter and
spent many a good lunchtime eating well from the
brash-fire embers and contemplating the old map
with local names, which called this piece of woodland
'Dirty Gate'. The ride naturally led to what would
seem a sensible place for a gate to enter the field
beyond. Near to that entrance the stream widens out
and crosses the ride, and it is a place that naturally
becomes muddy and might invoke the name 'Dirty
Gate'. We also surmised that it might have been a
popular place for young lovers to meet and that its
name may have been coined from this. The cottage at
Oaklands in view of Dirty Gate was once an ale house
and no doubt was a frequent haunt of coppice and
farm workers, for whom a stroll up to the woodland
may have been a popular pastime.

Coppice woodlands are full of history and the
stories of those who have worked them. One common
theme I've both heard of and come across in real life
is the literal meaning of 'hanging up your boots'. It
seems to be a tradition that coppice workers will
leave their boots in the last area (cant) that they cut.

I found a good, sturdy pair of leather boots beneath a coppice stool left to slowly disintegrate. I wonder which usually lasts longer: the retired coppice worker or his boots? And I wonder which cant I will leave my boots in. I don't plan to retire from cutting coppice and it is a way of life, not a job, but no doubt one day I'll know it's my last cant, and I shall leave my boots there and join the path of others before me.

Tools of the trade often appear in the copse. I once found a small bill hook wedged into a fork in a chestnut stem, and different forms of cleaving break to help with splitting chestnut appear all over the woods. These can be wooden rails nailed or lashed to trees with notches cut out of them, so that they resemble wooden teeth. I've also found a metal equivalent – an old Allen scythe blade fixed to a tree with a rail above that made a simple yet effective cleaving break. There were also the unwanted signs of previous coppice workers, the rusty cans and plastic bottles of chainsaw oil that are found in many woods. I cannot understand the mentality of enjoying the beauty of coppicing an ancient woodland and then littering it with cans rather than taking responsibility and carrying them out.

Old car tyres are often found. Sadly, I can only imagine they were brought into the woodland for

starting fires. The woods are full of dry kindling even when it has been raining, and the pollution from burning a car tyre is particularly unpleasant. Other common finds are sheets of corrugated iron. These are often brought in to heat up over a fire and warm frozen rods on a cold morning. The warming process frees up the fibres and allows the rod to become flexible again. Warming rods this way is popular with hurdle makers in hazel copses. The saying 'Leave only your footprints' is as relevant today as it was when it was first hailed.

Each year I cut a cant of coppice and now after 20 years it seems so natural a part of my life I cannot imagine a winter without the experience. It is during these winter months that so many ideas germinate as I fell materials that will be used throughout the following year to construct and make the products of my trade.

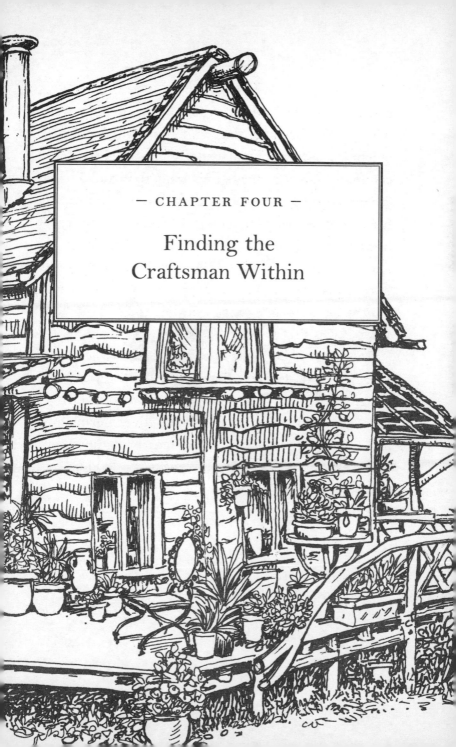

— CHAPTER FOUR —

Finding the
Craftsman Within

When I first started felling coppice, to begin with I naturally took the path well trodden when it came to adding value and making produce. I also needed to learn the basic craft skills that would enable me to use my imagination to create some new and unique markets.

A pole cut from the coppice has an initial value – if I point one end it becomes a fence post, and therefore a product. If I split it in half (cleave it), it becomes two posts and I am beginning to add value to the coppice I have cut. My early lessons in adding value were both lessons in learning about the nature of the wood I was working with and the basic economics of sustaining a livelihood from a coppiced woodland.

I clearly remember cleaving my first pole. It was a chestnut stem about 6 foot long and 6 inches in diameter, and I cleft it using two axe heads. I started at the thin end and found the very centre of the pole. When sweet chestnut first grows from the coppice stool it is not round; the first year of growth is star

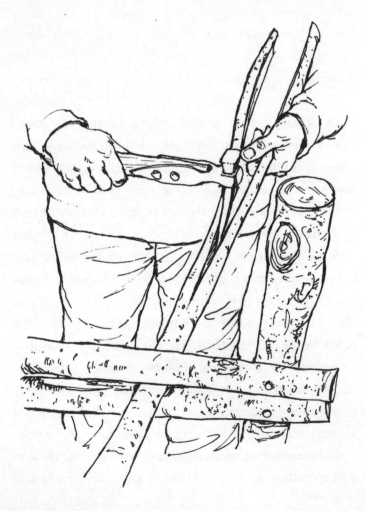

shaped. When you look at the very centre of the end grain of a chestnut pole, you will see a tiny star in the middle. The star is what I aim to split into two with the axe head. I remember, as I swung the maul, the first engagement of the steel penetrating the chestnut. It felt easier than I imagined and the second swing brought further satisfaction as the axe had embedded itself into the end of the pole and a distinct split opened up in front of it. After the third strike the split was far enough in front of the wedge (axe head) to place a second axe head into the opening split and drive that one with the maul. Soon the pattern of putting one wedge in front of the other and driving the split from one end of the pole to the other became an almost automatic process. A couple more strikes and the pole parted to form a mirrored pair of half rounds. The first glimpse of the inner figure of that sweet chestnut pole was like a moment of alchemy. From a round, bark-covered pole I had unearthed the most beautiful, honey-coloured pattern of wood, which emitted a sweet, nostalgic perfume. It cried out for me to run my hand across its naked, riven face. I was the first to see this beautiful sight in its virginal glory. I had never seen such purity in a piece of wood. I had witnessed the birth of a plank and I had been the midwife.

With the pleasure of each end result, I cleaved feverishly through pole after pole. Each pole was a lesson. I learned how to work around the knots and how the straightness of the grain dictated the ease with which each pole cleaved. The ones that ran out before the split had completed the length of the pole were lessons, and I would conduct my own post-mortem into the causes of any run-out. This process produced an abundance of fence posts but above all began my learning process into the nature of sweet chestnut.

As I have mentioned, sweet or Spanish chestnut was brought to Britain by the Romans, adapted well, and is now regarded amongst foresters as an honorary native. It was planted in abundance in the mid-1800s to create poles for hop gardens to help fuel the English desire for beer and also to create material for fencing. The south-east, the main hop-growing region in the country, became home to acres of sweet chestnut coppice. There now stands about 18,000 hectares of sweet chestnut coppice, the majority in Sussex, Surrey and Kent, an abundant resource managed by past generations to leave us with a wealth of useful poles to adapt to our needs in the 21st century. To those who planted these vibrant coppices, I am eternally grateful.

As I have worked sweet chestnut as both a coppice worker and a woodworker, there are particular qualities that make it stand out. The first must be its ability to cleave. Sweet chestnut wants to split and this ability opens up the opportunity for a range of cleft products. The process of cleaving that forces the fibres apart keeps much of the strength of the original pole, and far more than had it been sawn. In a chestnut 'shake' or 'shingle', the cleft face sheds water as opposed to a sawn face, which invites the cut fibres to act like a sponge and suck moisture into the wood.

Another fine quality of sweet chestnut is its natural durability resulting from the large amounts of tannic acid contained within it – hence its favoured use for fence posts. This natural durability, similar to that of oak, allows the coppice worker to produce a range of products from sweet chestnut with the confidence that they will last.

Added to its durability is sweet chestnut's ability to produce heartwood at a very young age. A pole of sweet chestnut rarely has more than four years of sapwood, resulting in poles of a small diameter of which a large part is the durable heartwood.

Yet another of its qualities is its tremendous speed of growth. Most of the coppiced stools I cut put on six to eight feet of re-growth in the first year. This is particularly important as it means it grows beyond deer-grazing height in its first year.

The last fine quality of sweet chestnut I want to mention is the nuts themselves, cleverly encased in a spiky case, which keeps the squirrels at bay until they are ripe and beginning to fall. This nut, low in fat but high in protein, is an important staple in some countries.

When I first spent my year of observation at Prickly Nut Wood, I was only aware of a few qualities and uses of sweet chestnut. Now, 20 years later, I cannot praise highly enough this productive coppice tree.

Having mastered cleaving the six-foot fence post, I moved onto cleaving rails. Sweet chestnut post and rail fencing is the vernacular style in Sussex and the market for the rails is fairly constant. The rails are cleaved out of coppiced sweet chestnut of 30 to 35 years of age, producing poles of around 11 to 13 inches diameter at the butt. These poles are then crosscut into ten-foot lengths and then cleaved into quarters. This involves first cleaving the pole in half, and then each half is cleaved to create the four quarters. These rails are trimmed at each end to form a rustic tenon that inserts into the mortise. Part of the charm is that the rails are often not straight, and slightly curvy rails can be matched as pairs one above the other in a bay in the fence. Keeping these curvy pieces ensures more rails and more return to the coppice worker, but also can test the skills of the woodsman and his ability to read the pole before cleaving. As the cleaving becomes more difficult, the use of wedges has its limitations as there is little control in bringing the split back into line once it begins to run off. This calls for a cleaving break.

10 March

Today I set out with a plan for making some chestnut pales. Partly because I need some pales, but also to experience cleaving with a froe and cleaving break. I made a simple cleaving break in the copse by high-cutting two poles, leaving about six foot of growth from the stool, and on to these I fixed two cross poles. The cross poles I fixed on top of each other where they attached to the first six-foot upright, and then they opened up and attached to each side of the other six-foot pole. The cross poles formed a narrow triangle. This allowed me to insert a range of different-sized poles into the break. I knocked the end of my froe into the sweet chestnut round and at first the split ran centrally, but as I worked the froe further

*into the pole the split began to run off. I placed the pole
into the vice of the cleaving brake and inserted my
hand into the split and pressed down on the thicker
side of the split whilst levering with the froe. This
caused the split that was running out to return to its
original central course. At last I have a method to
control the cleave. This feels like a eureka moment. I
now feel confident in my ability to cleave poles at a
good pace, and in doing so to add value to this coppice
resource. I'm touched by the ease with which the splits
can be returned and re-centred and how responsive the
wood is to my touch. Amazing to think how coppice
workers devised such simple yet effective brakes and
how many have been in use across the chestnut coppices
in the south-east.*

Having mastered cleaving with a froe, I wanted to
master cleaving small-diameter poles with a cleaving
adze. These small adzes are traditional in Sussex and
I have had a few made up by local blacksmiths. The
best was probably the one forged by David Wright of
Chiddingfold forge. This is a beautiful cleaving adze,
but is a little large for cleaving one- to one-and-a-
half-inch chestnut poles. I have two very small adzes
made for me by Steve Darby of Green Man Ironwork.
Although the finish is not as fine as David Wright's,

the light weight of this adze makes it perfect for cleaving small rods for hurdle panels. When cleaving a small rod with a cleaving adze I start by splitting the star in the thin end of the rod and working down the rod using the adze. Once it begins to run out, I place the rod in the break and in inserting my fingers into the cleave, I put downward pressure on the thick side of the cleave and it soon begins to correct itself. After awhile, the clicking sound of the adze working its way down the rod becomes so familiar that any run-off can almost be gauged by the change in sound. After a couple of days of cleaving this way, the feel and process will be almost automatic and it will be rare that a cleave runs out.

With the ability to cleave chestnut from small rods of less than an inch diameter up to large logs, it was time to make a range of products to sell.

*   *   *

The market for hurdles has remained good, despite the fact that their traditional use for folding or penning sheep has now disappeared. The attractiveness of the wattle hurdle has meant that it is a coppice staple through sales into the garden sector. Different parts of the country have their own particular styles and weaves of hurdle, but it is rare that I have good-quality hazel for hurdle making. Most of my hazel is obtained from restoring derelict coppice, and beyond that I use chestnut. With both poor-quality hazel and chestnut I make panels rather than hurdles as they use shorter lengths of poorer-quality material and in my opinion produce a more durable alternative to the traditional hazel hurdle. The panels I make consist of sweet chestnut posts about 4 inches in diameter and then cleft chestnut posts of similar size to form the top and bottom of the panel. The curve of the half round faces outwards from the panel and helps protect the woven material, keeping it off the ground and protected with a capping. Between the two half rounds I place chestnut zales. The half rounds are drilled top and bottom, and the zales are bent into place. The split hazel or chestnut for the weave is woven around the zales. This produces a durable, attractive panel and makes good use of the materials I have available. Most years I have a number of orders for these panels and they continue to be a good revenue stream.

Working with such a durable timber as chestnut, a continuous flow of ideas arises in me as to what to make from the coppice poles. This varies from simply rustic furniture ideas through to more complex projects. One design I worked on in the early days was a chestnut seat with a rose arbour above. I used a forked chestnut stem (or a prog) and matching curves each side of the prog to create an interesting back to the seat. The seat itself was a couple of chestnut planks. These I hewed out of a large chestnut pole using a long-handled carpenter's adze. After constructing the first of these seats, I photographed the end result and marketed it as a product to be made to order. I soon realised that selling it as a chestnut seat with rose arbour was long-winded and not eye-catching. When I re-marketed the product as a loveseat, the number of orders quickly increased. I learned my first lesson in marketing.

As much as I work out patterns and designs for rustic furniture, when you are working with the natural forms and shapes of trees the opportunity to build free-form should not be ignored. Sometimes reacting spontaneously and going with what feels right can produce a unique item. An example of this happened in the summer of 2000. I had been making bentwood chairs with my then apprentices Anthony and Ele Waters, and we had been carefully constructing seats and curve patterns for the backs. We had all been out to the Hollist Arms and had quite a celebratory party night, during which beer and tequila slammers had been consumed. The following day was a Sunday and we all rose for breakfast a little hungover. After some coffee and breakfast I suggested to Anthony that we build a free-form chair. We both grabbed pieces of hazel and randomly nailed on the pieces in an irregular pattern. The chair stood out from the others with its quirky style and we named it the 'tequila chair'. The next day was Bank Holiday Monday and we went to the village recreation ground to set up stall at the annual village fête. The fête had not long been open when a man offered to buy a pair of bentwood chairs. When I asked which two he would like, he chose an elegant bentwood design and the tequila chair. I learnt two lessons from this process: the first, to allow free-form to play a part in creating your designs; the second, to transform the state of mind that a hangover can create into a creative opportunity. So, if I ever rise with a hangover, rather than waste a day of my life complaining about how I feel, I engage with the day and take it as a creative opportunity. The slightly trancelike feeling one has of not being fully in the world is an opportunity that can be harnessed for creative expression.

*   *   *

When I first started 20 years ago, as well as my desire to deepen my knowledge of the woods, I was driven by a dislike of how much unsustainable timber we import. One area of the market I was interested in was charcoal. Charcoal is a traditional coppice product, yet at the time 98 per cent of what was consumed in the UK was imported. This imported charcoal for the most part was coming from environmentally degraded landscapes, such as rainforest and mangrove swamps. Charcoal burning seemed a good area in which to begin, especially when I had so much derelict coppice and at the time a limited knowledge of how to market it.

To learn the basics of charcoal burning, I went on a course at the Weald and Downland Open Air Museum. The museum, situated near to me at the foot of the South Downs in Singleton, has been an inspiration and a place I regularly visit. It has been established for 40 years, and in its beautiful setting has collected and reconstructed on-site traditional buildings and artefacts from the countryside of the Weald. It also runs a number of courses in traditional crafts and building skills. At the time the museum's charcoal burner was Alan Waters. Alan has been working in and out of hazel coppice for a number of years, and currently runs his own company making

coppice products. He has revived the Sussex 'pimp', a circular bundle of kindling referred to by Herbert Edlin in his classic text, *Woodland Crafts in Britain*.

The one-day course with Alan was informative and gave many pointers, but was limited in the amount of practical experience I was able to gain from it. Then Alan offered me the opportunity to work with him at the museum if I was serious about charcoal burning. I grasped this opportunity and joined him at the museum, and whilst unloading a kiln he answered some of my many questions. I ordered my first kiln from Bryan Wilson, who runs a forge in Mid-Wales. I still have that kiln and although the steel has worn through in places, it is still operational. Bryan is still making quality charcoal kilns and I purchased another from him recently.

I clearly remember my first burn. I levelled a hearth to place the kiln on and stockpiled the soil for earthing-up. I then positioned the steel inlets and sat the kiln on top of them. I had a pile of well-seasoned chestnut, varying in diameter from about three to seven inches. I laid out some of the larger pieces to create the cartwheel pattern at the base that allows a clear flow of air through the inlets to the centre of the fire. I then split some of the larger pieces in half with an axe and laid them on top of the cartwheel pieces to close off the inlets, forming tunnels at the base of the kiln. I then added a little kindling in the centre and began to load the kiln, packing the pieces of wood in as tightly as possible like a giant, circular jigsaw. The larger pieces I placed in the centre and the smaller ones towards the outside and the top. After a few hours of sawing, splitting and packing, the kiln was full and I chocked up the lid with a few small logs that I could remove at the appropriate time in the burn to allow the lid to close.

With the kiln filled it was time to light my first burn. I remember the slightly nervous feeling of lighting my first kiln in the woods and the large fire I was about to create. My mind wandered to the many charcoal burners of the past who had eked out a living from making charcoal without the luxury of a steel kiln to control the blaze and breakout of the fire. Their lives had been hard. They lived with their families in huts in the woodlands where they worked, staying up many nights to tend and control the fire as it smouldered and tried to break through the turf and soil piled on to the blaze. The charcoal burner's chair was a one-legged stool, designed so that if you fell asleep you would fall off, awakening you. It was meant to keep you vigilant at all times, as your livelihood could easily burn away.

With the relative ease of the task ahead now placed in perspective, I collected a bucket of red-hot embers from the outdoor kitchen fire and, armed with a pair of gauntlets, a shovel and a crowbar, I made my way to light my first burn. I emptied the bucket of embers by two of the air inlets and, using a thin stick, pushed the embers into the centre of the kiln so they rested amongst the kindling. With the draw of air through the tunnelled vents, it was not long before the kindling caught alight from the embers in the fire. The initial few minutes produced the reassuring sounds of crackling as the kindling ignited, and then the first swirls of smoke started to emerge from the gap between the chocked-up lid and the kiln. As the minutes passed, the intensity of the crackling sound increased, as did the smoke, thick and white, which flowed out of the kiln and up into the sky. The whole kiln began to resemble a huge cauldron in which some magical concoction was brewing.

What was occurring was the first steps in the process of the distillation of wood. The fire continued to burn and spread from the centre to the edges of the kiln. As the fire reached the outside edge of the kiln, and red embers were clearly visible between the air inlets, I earthed up the air gap at the bottom of the kiln between the inlets to move the fire around.

Soon I was earthing up between more inlets and it was not long before the inlets were all that was left visible. Next, I placed the chimneys on alternative inlets and earthed up around them, turning the inlets into outlets. Usually there is an immediate roar as the chimney begins to draw and the smoke begins to appear out of the chimneys, as well as the still-open gap between the lid and the kiln. Next, I removed the chocks from between the lid and the kiln, and the lid closed the kiln. This usually coincides with a loud hiss, flames shooting out of the inlets, and a ring of fire that burns off the gases often appearing around the top and the bottom of the kiln. This is a spectacular moment in the charcoal-burning process and, although a little unpredictable, is a moment all charcoal burners look forward to. After a few minutes the gases burned themselves out and I shovelled more earth over the lid; using the gauntlets I pushed the soil into the seal where the lid and kiln met. The process of earthing-up the lid and the base between the inlets gives a small level of continuity to traditional charcoal burners who did not have steel kilns, and relied totally on earthing-up to control their burns and would be far more busy throughout the burn. At this point the kiln was under control and could be left for a period to settle into its slow-burning routine. The fire was still burning within the kiln with a restricted supply of oxygen, the end result being a product of almost pure carbon.

I usually return to the kiln about an hour later to check all the chimneys are puffing well and the inlets are drawing in sufficient air. The kiln seems almost orderly at this stage. The chaos of the cauldron of swirling white smoke is transformed into upright pillars of smoke and glowing inlets below. Weather conditions can have a major impact on the outcome of a charcoal burn, as well as the amount of time that I need to spend with the kiln. If the wind picks up, I may need to spend a lot of time changing chimneys and inlets to ensure that the burn remains more even. This may entail many visits at night. Even on a still night I always visit the kiln to swap inlets and chimneys once, to ensure an even burn and maximise the volume of finished charcoal. This is always a special visit and often I will sit with the kiln for a while, watching the plumes of smoke against the moonlight and the warm, orange glow emitting from the inlets below. Sitting quietly beside a warm kiln in the middle of the night when most people are sleeping, in the middle of an English woodland, is a unique experience. The woods come alive at night and on most visits I will hear, if not see, nocturnal woodland life in action.

21 June

I find myself on the shortest night sitting around the kiln, surveying this woodland scene I know so well. I have moved the kiln to 'captains', and I'm beginning to work through some of the piles of chestnut we stacked two years ago when we re-coppiced this area and cleared the rhododendron. I love the way my ears wake up when it is dark and how I can discern small scratchings and rustlings that I would easily miss during the daylight. The sound of the smallest creature is so amplified in the dark because we really listen. I wish I could listen as well during the day. The kiln has burnt well tonight, nice and even, and should supply enough bags for the wood fair. Estimate there is enough wood for about another 10 burns up at captains – should be enough to see out this summer, unless it turns into a heat wave. Disturbed a badger on my return home.

About twelve hours after lighting the kiln (using a 6-foot-diameter ring kiln), it is time to close it down. As I tend to light my kilns in the early evening so that they burn through the night and the smoke is not a nuisance to neighbours, it is usually early morning when I close down the kilns. Arriving on a summer's morning, when the warmth of the day has not yet emerged, to be greeted by birdsong and the warmth of the kiln, now emitting slow wisps of smoke from its chimneys, is a thought-provoking way to begin one's day. The smoke will have lost its white colour and now be almost translucent, perhaps a shade of metallic blue. I remove all the chimneys and cover over all the inlets with soil, completely sealing the kiln and shutting off all intake of oxygen. All that will be left will be a heat haze over the lid of the kiln. The kiln is left like this to cool for two days before opening. If opened too early, the oxygen could re-ignite the kiln. Opening the kiln is always an exciting moment. Although I have by now made enough charcoal to be pretty certain how well the burn has gone by how the kiln behaved during the burn, the truth is only revealed when I open the lid. The first view gives an initial sense of the burn. If the wind got up during the night the inlet channels may have burnt away a lot of wood. If there are a lot of brown ends (partly converted logs) it shows I either shut the kiln down too early or failed to get the fire to spread out to the edges of the kiln. Instinct makes me pick up a piece of charcoal every time I open a kiln. The weight and sound are familiar. It is time to bag up.

My first burn was reasonably successful and I've improved my techniques to refine the process into a reliable method for producing charcoal for barbecues. When I first started marketing the charcoal, I had some bags printed explaining the local origins of the charcoal, how it is produced, the fact that the wood used to make the charcoal came from coppice woodlands and the importance of the sustainable management of these woodlands. This was far too much information and I've now simplified the packaging to a few key words. Recent research carried out on charcoal packaging concluded that the key information the public wants on a bag of charcoal is that it 'lights easily and burns hot'.

To see how interest has grown in locally produced charcoal, I have only to mention my trading with one small, local ironmongery, whom I first approached to sell charcoal to in 1993. It was an April morning when I met with the manager and explained about the charcoal I was producing, and its benefits over the imported charcoal he had for sale in his shop. After a look at the product and packaging – and a lot of pushing from me – he said he would take half a dozen bags on sale or return. About two weeks later, I called in at the shop to see how they were selling and not a single bag had sold. 'Better take them away. Can't see them selling here.'

I wore that disappointment for a couple of years, while I sold direct to the public and built up a few other retail outlets. About two years later I got a call from the manager of the local hardware store, explaining he had received a request for local charcoal and could I supply him with 20 bags. I delivered them, and it was not long before a second 20 were ordered. Now another 16 years on, I am the sole charcoal supplier for the hardware shop and they no longer sell imported charcoal. This clearly shows that the buyer is becoming more discerning and more people are willing to pay a little extra to get a good-quality local product.

I also make artists' charcoal. I do this by peeling thin twigs and placing them in a biscuit tin. I pack the biscuit tin with sawdust, pierce a couple of holes in the lid and then tie the lid on with a piece of wire. I place the biscuit tin inside the charcoal kiln to the outside, near the top and midway between the inlets, and it converts to charcoal with the contents of the rest of the kiln.

I began by making the charcoal from willow, as this was what I knew was commercially available, but it was not long before I experimented with other woods. Research led me to try oak and spindle and, being surrounded by it, I had of course to try sweet chestnut. The results from all the different woods were good; different woods gave different shades and textures, which were gratefully received by artists.

In the early 1990s Rodney Baldwin, who runs Green & Stone art supplies in the Kings Road, Chelsea, lived in Lodsworth and he contacted me about purchasing some artists' charcoal for his shop. I remember putting some makeshift packaging together. I used a paper bread wrapper to wrap up the charcoal and then cut out a brown paper envelope to go over the top of the bread wrapper. I tied it up with a piece of sisal and hand wrote on the packaging: 'Artists' charcoal, 12 sticks mixed diameter, produced in the woods, Prickly Nut Wood, Lodsworth'. When I took the charcoal down to Rodney's house, I apologised about the packaging and told him I was getting some boxes printed. Rodney replied, 'No, don't do that. This packaging is just right.' So I cancelled my box order and to this day I package my artists' charcoal in old bread wrappers, cut-out brown envelopes and sisal! Another marketing lesson learned.

Since my early making of artists' charcoal, I have seen the possibility and demand for a range of English wood charcoal. A selection of different trees would without doubt produce a fine range of different-textured charcoals. It is hard to find commercial alternatives to willow, and although willow makes a fine charcoal, grows in straight rods and is often made in association with basket making or hurdle making, and is therefore a by-product of that industry, there are many other woods that make fine artists' charcoal and give a wider variety of textures and tones.

Every charcoal burner I know who burns in the woods using a portable ring kiln leaves behind piles of what we call charcoal 'fines' – small pieces that have fallen through the riddles at bagging time. What to do with these piles has been a concern of mine for a number of years. In the mid-1990s, a group of us looked into the possibility of selling the charcoal fines to a charcoal filtration company. However, our investigations revealed that the charcoal must be dry, free from contaminants and at an easy-to-access collection point. Our fines, however, are contaminated with leaves and bird droppings, are often far from an easy collection point, and a dry storage space would be out of the question. Dry storage spaces in woodland life are far too valuable to fill up with charcoal fines. So the idea was abandoned. But then along came biochar.

Biochar came to public notice after a television documentary about the dark soils of the Amazon region (the so-called *terra preta*). These rich, dark soils were fertile and productive, and the origins of this lay in the use of charcoal dust. Charcoal does not act as a fertiliser; it is actually inert but it works like a type of sponge, retaining moisture, and allowing microbes and fungi to colonise it. In James Bruges's book, *The Biochar Debate*, he quotes Chris Turney, professor of geography at Exeter University, saying that 'biochar's porous structure is ideal for trapping nutrients and beneficial microorganisms that help plants grow. It also improves drainage and can prevent up to 80 per cent of greenhouse gases such as nitrous oxide and methane from escaping from the soil.' Biochar production can be made from any organic material, but for those of us already burning charcoal and sitting on piles of charcoal fines, there is a ready market for our fines. Charcoal is almost pure carbon and by burying it in the soil we are locking up that carbon. Charcoal does not break down in the soil; deposits have been discovered dating back thousands of years, so the burying of charcoal has to be a useful tool in helping to re-stabilise our planet.

I know of a couple of charcoal burners in Northumberland who have been selling biochar to the Royal Botanic Garden in Edinburgh and who are finding that the demand for biochar is beginning to outstrip the demand for barbecue charcoal. It would feel good to know that a good percentage of the fines we are producing in charcoal production was returning to the earth in the form of biochar.

The coppice at Prickly Nut Wood is now restored and on cycle, and I am no longer cutting coppice to make charcoal. I cut coppice for other products and the waste wood from these products then becomes charcoal. Hence my charcoal burning is now creating a product out of a waste product. If I go and build a pergola or some fencing for a client, the off-cuts come back with me and join the piles of timber for charcoal. Similarly, if wood I have coppiced has not been used for other purposes, after two to three years it is then converted into charcoal.

Having learnt some basic craft skills and understood the nature and properties of the wood I work with through working in the coppice, the next stage for me was to specialise – finding a niche, something unique, something that others had not yet tried. The opportunities in niche markets are everywhere. We just need to open our imagination and then create and market the product. For me, my niche unexpectedly came from building and the linking of coppice products into the building industry.

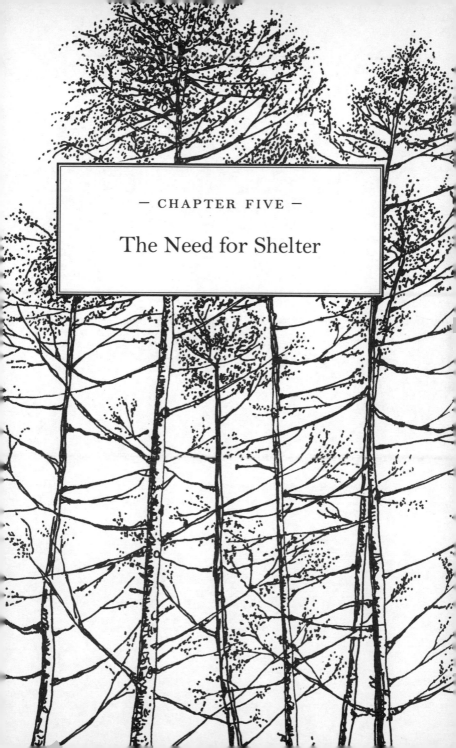

CHAPTER FIVE

The Need for Shelter

S helter, a roof over our head, is a basic human need. How and what we build a shelter from will vary considerably, depending upon where on the planet we live. If we study local architecture, it is clear that the use of the available local resources has dictated how buildings have evolved. Taking the United Kingdom at a local level, we soon notice that where there is a clay soil, bricks, cob and clay tiles are abundant; in the chalk regions we find lime and flint; and where it is heavily forested, more timber is used. In recent years this pattern has changed. Architects design buildings and then search for the resources to meet their designs, using materials that have been transported vast distances across the globe at great environmental cost. The need for architects to start with a study of available local resources and then design from what is to hand has never been more

necessary. Wood is often transported from Russia to be used on a building in Sussex, when there is perfectly suitable material growing a few hundred yards away from the building site. We must start to use our own resources and manage them sustainably so there are materials for future generations to use. In doing so, we must design suitable buildings that can incorporate locally grown timbers.

My first dwellings at Prickly Nut Wood were timber and canvas. Provided a wood burner kept them dry and warm in the winter, these were suitable as basic, year-round dwellings. A 'bender' has the advantage of being able to be constructed in a single day. A number of freshly cut hazel poles, some twine and a canvas tarpaulin – and you have a shelter. For all-year-round living, there are a number of extras that turn such a shelter into a comfortable home. A raised floor is important, especially during winter. I made a raised floor from a collection of pallets and then boarded over them. A rug over the top and you have a dry floor, raised up and ideal for winter living. A good-sized window makes a huge difference on wet winter days, as does a comfortable chair, and I always like a door frame and a wooden door. Canvas doors are frustrating to tie back and to anchor securely shut.

My second dwelling was a yurt. Yurts are beautiful structures and well designed to withstand extreme weather. I made my first yurt with the knowledge that there was a baby on the way, and the need for the yurt to be finished for us to begin family life in a new home was always pressing. I cut the roof poles (ribs) and wall poles (trellis) from five-year-old sweet chestnut coppice, and peeled them all with a draw knife. I then oiled the trellis poles and drilled out the holes for the cord to tie the lattice work together. 560 holes to drill. This was a time when cordless drills did not feature in an average tool kit, so a small hand twist drill did all the work. The roof ribs needed bending. I boil bent them by placing a 40-gallon drum on top of some bricks so that I could light a fire beneath it and then filled it with water and placed the butt ends of the 42 roof ribs into the 'cauldron'. I then boiled these for an hour, before bending them over a jig created by a fallen tree to create a curve in the bottom section of the roof rib. They stayed in the bending jig for two days.

The hoop or ring of the yurt is one of its most beautiful features, and steam bending a perfect circle makes the aesthetics of the hoop feel balanced. For the hoop I cut a 15-foot length of sweet chestnut about five inches in diameter and around 16 years of age. I then cleaved the length with a froe to give me two

15-foot half rounds. I chose the best one and kept the other for a spare, in case the first one failed. I then worked my chosen half round with a draw knife to reduce the thickness down to about one and a half inches, and then placed it into my steam-bending tube. Steam bending is one of carpentry's more unusual processes. At the beginning of the day I can cut down a living stem of sweet chestnut and by the end of the day it has become a round hoop. The manipulation of the fibres within the timber is an extreme process, but the end result is incredibly satisfying. My steamer is made up from an army water boiler, but one can as be easily constructed from a raised 40-gallon oil drum, with a hole drilled in the lid from which a pipe runs to the tube where the timber to be steamed is placed. This tube is commonly made up from a large plastic pipe that can withstand pressure. Large gas main pipes work well; a poorer alternative is a plywood box or even a steel tube. The 15-foot yurt half round needs three hours of constant steaming. It is important to keep the fire burning at 'full throttle', for if it dies down and the level of steam is reduced, then much of the penetration of the fibres can be lost.

The simplest example of how steam bending works is to compare it to boiling spaghetti. When spaghetti is dry it is brittle – if you try to bend it, it will break.

Once it has been boiled it can be bent into a shape, and once it cools it sets into this shape. Wood is similar. The steaming soaks the fibres and allows them to be realigned; once cooled, the timber sets into its new position. Any steam bending relies on a solid former around which the steamed wood is bent. For the Yurt hoop, I used a four-foot-diameter iron-wheel tyre; such artefacts can often be found on farms in the countryside. To this some internal welding was carried out to strengthen it further for when the bending began. I like to have a least two other people on hand during the bending process, as there is only a short window of time in which to bend and clamp the timber onto the former. Before it was put into the steamer, I tapered down each end of the 15-foot piece so that the ends would overlap as they were bent around the former, completing a 360° hoop out of one piece of wood. When the piece of wood comes out of the steam box it must be swiftly carried to the former (gloves have to be worn, as the timber will be very hot!). And as one person bends it around the iron wheel, others follow behind, quickly clamping the timber to the iron wheel.

Once the hoop has been clamped in place, it is time to relax, stand back and appreciate the key component of the yurt – from growing tree to finished hoop in less than a day. The hoop stays on the former for about two days before it is removed. It is then pegged or bolted together. Soaked rawhide wrapped tightly around the tapered joint will shrink as it dries, and makes an attractive finish. The hoop is then drilled out 42 times to receive the roof ribs, then finished by heating up an old copper soldering iron in the fire and pushing it through the drilled holes. The soldering iron sizzles and smokes as it turns a round hole into a square one. The roof ribs are finished with square, tapered ends so that they cannot twist once inserted into the hoop. More holes are drilled for the hoop bracing. This forms both an attractive infill to the hoop but also works to brace the hoop, as pressure is applied on all sides of the hoop by the roof ribs both during raising and once the yurt is standing. A wooden threshold and door frame allow for a wooden door and complete the timber work. A canvas band that encircles the yurt from door frame to door frame, covering where the roof ribs sit in the horns of the trellis poles, acts as a structural part of the yurt. Like a bender, a woodland yurt benefits from a raised floor. Living in the round structure of the yurt, looking up through the circular wheel to the stars, was for me one of the many highlights of my woodland journey.

*   *   *

Around this time my existence at Prickly Nut Wood had reached the notice of the local planning authority. I arrived after a foraging outing to find an enforcement notice pinned to the yurt's canvas. An enforcement notice is quite a blunt correspondence and an insensitive approach as a point of first contact. I felt a sense of how an Amazonian forest dweller must feel when confronted by a logging company threatening their home. This enforcement notice was the beginning of a drawn-out dispute between myself and the local planning authority, one characterised by mistrust on both sides. In hindsight – and with a deeper understanding of planning law on my part – they were just doing their job. The approach they took in carrying out their actions, however, was insensitive and likely to provoke a reaction in anyone whose home was threatened.

My frustration boiled up from not being able to explain the bigger picture as to why I was living in the woods. The forest dweller's approach to life and work, and the deeper understanding of the landscape, all seemed to have no place within planning law and I felt as a woodlander carrying out a tradition of land use and forest dwelling rather persecuted by the bureaucracy of planning law. I think the rather aggravated poem I wrote at the time sums it up rather well.

who are you o suited one
who walks upon this land
straight from your BMW
with clipboard in your hand
you have come to inspect a landscape
you will never understand
you question why I'm living here
and the structures in which I dwell
and then report back to a muddle of heads
in a landscape I call hell
remember we are men of wood and steel
with bill hooks of razor edge
that slice through grain of chestnut
and plash a rambling hedge
remember when you talk to me
I am married to the land
and whoever crosses my path this life
these words should understand

I had been living on the land for over three years. If that had increased to four years without any action being taken, I could have been in a position to claim a lawful development certificate. At the time, however, I knew nothing of this. I knew that charcoal burners and woodsman had often lived simply in the woods, and considering that planning law only came into being in 1948, these woodland practices clearly preceded it.

After appealing against the enforcement order and losing my appeal, I put in an application for planning permission for a mobile home and gained temporary planning permission for three years. It is normal practice to be given three years for agricultural/ forestry enterprises to see if they are viable. In order to achieve planning permission on the land you have two 'tests' to pass. The first is the economic viability of the enterprise. I submitted accounts and business forecasts that I managed to meet and exceed during my three years' temporary permission. The second test is the essential need test. On agricultural land, it is accepted that it is an essential need to be on the land to look after livestock. But with forestry, the essential need was not so clear to the authorities, although it was obvious enough to me. Charcoal burning and tending charcoal fires at night within a woodland is clearly an essential need. This is supported by the need to not commute to work, as well as the wide range of produce and activities at Prickly Nut Wood that make it like a woodland farm, and therefore in need of day and night attention.

As my three years' temporary permission neared its end, I was already planning how to build a dwelling that would sit lightly in the sensitive woodland environment of Prickly Nut Wood. I wanted to build a timber house and I wanted to use sweet chestnut coppice. (I had no idea at this time that my interest in building with roundwood and natural materials would become a niche market and a key component of my future work.)

I had experimented in the building of a small boat-house and picked up the idea of a 'cruck frame'. This traditional timber frame is a fairly primitive type of 'A' frame and I could see its potential when building with round poles. I was fortunate to spend three years living in a mobile home on the very spot I would be building the house. This gave me plenty of time to work out the movement of the sun and how I wanted to orientate doors and windows. I drew up designs, and then contracted architect John Rees to draw them up to planning application standard and submit the drawings to the planners. My planning application was met with a fair amount of resistance, as it was without doubt a controversial application. I had a dialogue with the case officer (then the chief enforcement officer) and we discussed how we could allow me to continue to live and work at Prickly Nut Wood but avoid any risk of land speculation. We came up with personal conditions that allowed the dwelling for my lifetime, provided I continued to burn charcoal and run a woodland business of coppicing at Prickly Nut Wood. The dwelling was therefore legally tied to me personally and would be removed in the event of my death, or if I stopped the charcoal burning and coppice management activities. With such conditions tied to the planning application to safeguard against land speculation, the committee approved the application and building could begin. I was happy with the conditions, as it was essential to me that any dwelling was tied to the management of the woods.

*   *   *

The building of the woodland house at Prickly Nut Wood was a journey within my own life's journey and one of the most rewarding experiences of my life. When you have spent ten years drawing water from a well, then heating up the water over a fire for every shower and every bowl of washing-up water, the thought of hot, running water and a warm home where clothes stay dry and papers do not get damp and mouldy seems like a vast leap into an unimaginable future. There is also the primal, instinctive sense of building one's nest. I had roamed the forest for ten years and it was time to create my shelter. I had no idea that this way of building would become a niche market for me in the future and that I was embarking on building the prototype of a new architectural vernacular.

I was excited about the building process. My caravan roof had so many holes in it, I was now harvesting buckets of rainwater on the inside. All around the buckets I covered the walls of the caravan with sheets of flipchart paper on which I planned and managed the build. These sheets covered all the details and eventualities that I, who had never built a house before, could imagine. Of course, there were a few things I missed, but for a first attempt I did pretty well. I knew the build could work really successfully as a teaching tool for the sustainable building unit in permaculture courses, and I wanted to film it for this purpose. I arranged the filming but the company pulled out at the last moment on account of other commitments, and I was left four weeks before the build was due to start with no one to film it.

I then contacted Hugh Fearnley-Whittingstall, with whom I had filmed a rather fun charcoal burning and birch sap wine tapping scene on his *Cook on the Wild Side* series, the predecessor to his various *River Cottage* programmes. I knew he had his own film company and wondered if he would help. Hugh told me that I should contact *Grand Designs*. Not having a TV at the time, I did not know what *Grand Designs* was. (For anyone reading who is in the same position, *Grand Designs* is a long-running Channel 4 documentary series on people building or having built their dream homes, presented by Kevin McCloud.) Hugh mentioned he was going to be at a party at the weekend and would run into some of the producers from *Grand Designs*. He said he would put in a word for me.

True to his word he did just that and the following week I was contacted by *Grand Designs* about my project. A couple of weeks later we were filming. I think it helped that I knew nothing about *Grand Designs*, otherwise I might have questioned working on the programme with them. But, not having seen an episode until the programme on the 'Woodland House' was broadcast, I naively proceeded. I believe that not knowing what to expect helped maintain a relaxed atmosphere during the filming process. I remember the first piece I filmed, when Kevin McCloud asked me when it would be finished and I told him I would have to be in by winter. After all, my caravan would not survive as accommodation for another year. I think those words stayed with me and helped me to project-manage the build, with that timescale as my over-riding and necessary aim.

Although TV cameras can occasionally hold up progress, *Grand Designs* were very professional – Fiona, who directed the programme, and Nicole, who coordinated with me throughout, were great fun to have around. I enjoyed their company and I hope they enjoyed the whole experience as well. I doubt there are many TV crews who immediately understood that when they arrived at Prickly Nut Wood their first job was to break up some twigs, light the fire and get the kettle on. Nicole quickly picked up the skills. I knew the house I was building was unique and different, but to get the build filmed and put a message across to the mainstream via TV was an opportunity to profile sustainable building, forest management and so much of what I believe is vital for the future, as well as helping other eco-builders find a niche and gain wider acceptance for their work.

I had designed my build around a sweet chestnut cruck-frame barn, with lower-pitched roundwood box frames coming off the main aisle. I chose straw bales for my walling. Straw bales are an agricultural by-product and have such good insulation value they are an obvious choice. They complement a round-wood frame, as their depth – once lime-plastered – gives them the look of a solid stone wall. I've been intrigued by all aspects of lime plaster for years: the process of lime burning, the slightly macabre proposition of slaked lime and the wonderful breathability of the product, so vastly superior to modern-day concrete. (Concrete was a backwards step in building evolution, with so many buildings suffering where the use of concrete has trapped moisture – with lime it would have been able to escape and dry out.) I spent an interesting couple of days down in North Devon, where I attended a lime course with Mike Wye. The course was excellent in gaining the necessary confidence to proceed. So much of life is about confidence, and building a house (when you've never done it before) and having it filmed for TV needs a good amount of confidence.

I had planned on running the build using a large volunteer workforce. This was a risk, but I believed it was also an opportunity to empower people, give them the confidence that they too can build a house. During the build I had over 90 volunteers, the majority of whom turned out through word of mouth. It was a good summer and the word got round that there was this interesting build going on in the woods and it was a great place to be. In retrospect, when I am asked what that summer was like, I describe it thus: 'There was a carnival going on and in the background we put up a building.' As the project progressed I became more confident in my powers of delegation, and although the finished article carries a number of imperfections, there is a story to each one. When I sit by the fire and survey the timber frame I can remember who cut the tenons on the wall plates and why one on the veranda is a little rough – she had never held a chisel before. Although far from perfect, her work is good enough and I remember her every time I sit on the veranda and notice the imperfection. I hope she went back to Australia and built her own house as she planned. I look at the clay walls and I remember the hands that smoothed them over. This house is full of stories, full of people, and is built the way all houses should be built, by a community of people for a purpose.

The build began in early May, but I had prepared a lot of timber beforehand. I had felled larch trees from the plantation in the woods and with a mobile sawmill converted them into floor joists, roof rafters and stud work. I had also milled the oak from some of the thinned standards in the coppice into waney-edged boarding for the cladding. Other boards were sent away to be kiln dried in preparation for being turned into floorboards. I had felled some ash, which I had cleaved into two halves and then worked down with a side axe the previous year. This I took to Tim

Boxley's workshop in nearby Heyshott, where we machined it to the appropriate size. I left it with Tim to join together to create the window frames. The chestnut shingles were cleft out and in bundles, ready to be pre-drilled for nailing to the roof with copper clout nails. The straw bales had been baled the previous year and were sitting in a barn, where they were compressing and settling. The lime was made into putty and ready to mix. All of these activities were carefully marked on the flipchart sheets on the wall of my leaky caravan.

The sweet chestnut poles were all felled and piled up in the clearing near to the construction site. I colour-coded and marked them all for their appropriate use within the construction of the timber frame, and the process of peeling them was ongoing throughout the build. When a volunteer first arrived I would start them off on pole peeling. Partly because we had a lot of poles to peel, but also as it is a low-skilled job in which a volunteer will gain confidence and succeed in his or her task. It would give me time to assess their skill level and give them time to settle into the ambience of the project in the woods.

The foundation stones I had collected from all around the parish. It is amazing how many people have a few York stone slabs at the end of the garden when you ask. I put the word out on the local grape-vine that I needed foundation pad stones and over 40 stones turned up. Not wanting to use any concrete, I based my foundations upon pits filled with compacted sandstone from a local quarry and then placed a levelled York stone slab on top. The building then sat on top of the stones. This is a design I have continued to use on subsequent buildings. The only changes I have made are to place a piece of slate between the bottom of the pole and the York stone slab, which is then trimmed to the profile of the bottom of the pole, and to paint the bottom of the pole with a natural asphalt product – basically wood tar – to seal the end grain of the pole. These two additions improve the protection of contact between the pole and the foundation stone.

As well as ensuring all materials were sourced and prepared, there was the bureaucratic side of the building to sort out. Getting planning permission was one part of the building process, but building regulations threw up another range of problems to overcome. My foundations needed to be justified by an engineer, as did the timber frame design I was using. This, of course, added to the expected cost of the tight budget I was working with. I had already cut all the timber poles so I had to await the engineer's verdict. As I expected, all the poles I had cut were judged suitable for the timber frame I was building. Having engaged John Rees to submit my drawings, I now used his experience to deal with the building-control questions, while I concentrated on building the house.

I worked on the foundations with Stuart Cameron, an experienced digger operator who lives in the village. Stuart dug out the holes and I back-filled them with rubble and compacted them using a 'Jumping Jack' whacker. This vibrating whacker is the most suitable tool for compacting in a small area and, although unpleasant to use, it does an excellent job. I then levelled each pad stone on top of the compacted stone and within two days my foundations were complete. Using a builder's level I could then survey all the stones, working out the difference in millimetres between each of them and adjusting the height of each pole of the frame accordingly as it was constructed.

The next main job was peeling the main framing poles. Once we had a reasonable number peeled, we constructed a framing bed. A framing bed is a level platform upon which the frames of the house are made. It is constructed by digging short poles into the ground and then fixing cross members at regular intervals to form a level bed. I used 6-inch by 2-inch larch timbers to form the cross members, which then became floor joists once the framing bed was finished with. By using the framing bed as a map with all the key positions marked onto it, it is possible to joint a frame, remove it and then start on the next frame by using the marks on the framing bed to create a mirror image of the first frame. With all the timber for the mainframes peeled and jointed, the raising day approached.

The raising of my house at Prickly Nut Wood was the first of many raises that I have undertaken and

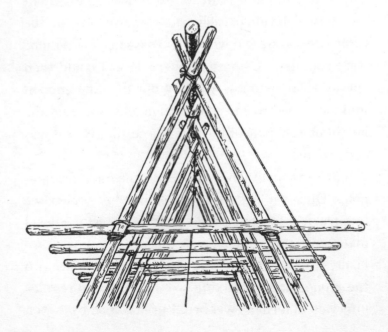

since that first raise, as with many parts of our building technique, we have refined the process. There is something truly satisfying about raising a house with a hand winch, ropes and human labour. This unique practice has become part of the fascination with roundwood timber framing. Traditionally, all timber frames would have been raised this way in the days before cranes, and what pleasure and sense of satisfaction does a crane bring? Will we be able to maintain and run machines such as cranes in a world with diminishing oil supplies? Raising days are exciting – they are the big moment early in the build. All the work that has taken place on the framing bed now appears in front of you, and the skeleton of the building stands up. It is also an occasion when everyone wants to be involved, and people can often become quite overexcited. Which makes the focus of the day all the more intense.

My role in these raises is to keep everyone focused. The raise itself is like a military operation. Everyone has an assigned task and knows their job; I limit the numbers, give a clear briefing and the raise goes on in silence. In our modern world of obsession over health and safety, in which adventure and risk are being bred out of our consciousness, it is all the more pleasurable to raise timber frame buildings this way, even if the risk assessment and method statement I have to submit takes almost as long to put together as jointing a frame! The satisfaction gained from frame raising – and the usual party and celebration which follows – are part of the joy of building we seem to have lost. If you travel the globe, you will find many cultures in which building a house is an important part of community life, and many friends and family members will come and help with house-building tasks. We seem to have lost the celebration and bringing together of community that house building brings. We seem to have lost the personal touch, and perhaps only self-build projects in the UK retain some of these elements. One practice we carry on at the roundwood timber-framing company is to encourage house owners to winch up their own house. This makes the project so much more real and makes the client, who has contracted us to build a house for them, more aware and engaged in the process. When, eventually, they live in the house, they can sit back proudly and say, 'I raised this house.'

During the build of the woodland house I fed large numbers of volunteers. I did most of the cooking myself, as it seemed right to cook for those who were helping me to build my house. After a good meal we would often walk through the woods to the Lickfold Inn, where the social side of our building experience erupted into evenings of laughter.

I would be up before six the next morning. I was sleeping on a wooden platform in the chestnut tree above the outdoor kitchen, so waking early was never a problem. I would light the outdoor kitchen fire, get the kettle on and make the first pot of coffee. That early-morning space before others had risen was my essential thinking time; it was how I planned the day, and it is a space I still value. Early on a summer's morning, kettle on the fire, surveying the woodland scene, no one to interrupt my thoughts – the perfect way to start the day.

The build progressed smoothly over the summer, and the help from volunteers ebbed and flowed. TV filming continued steadily, but as the summer nights began to draw in and the sense of autumn approached I felt a quickening within me. This feeling is one I relate to instinct, going back to the time of a more basic hunter–gatherer lifestyle. Many species are affected in different ways by the changes in the seasons and the reduction of daylight. Migratory birds know it is time to fly south; domestic chickens moult and egg production slows down; sheep begin their oestrus cycle knowing it is the right time to

become pregnant so that their lambs born in the spring have the best chance of survival and growing on to be able to face the following winter; and deciduous trees prepare to shed their leaves as their sap flow reduces. So is it any wonder that the coming of autumn affects us as well? To me, the feeling is one of urgency. Like squirrels gathering nuts for the oncoming winter, I need to be sure my firewood is stacked and dry, and I am prepared for and have comfortable shelter for the winter ahead. This urgency was particularly keen during the building of my house, as my diary reveals.

8 September

I feel the quickening. It is around me all the time but most of all at the beginning and end of the day. The lack of light and the increasing dew highlight how unprepared I feel for this winter. The house has so preoccupied me and there's still so much to do. 11 more weeks and Channel 4 return for the final filming! The pressure is on. I need to rally the volunteers, get everyone to pick up the pace – there is still so much to do. I'm going to install the Rayburn and get it lit so there is some warmth in the house, especially as there are eight tonnes of wet lime going in over the next few weeks. We can then begin cooking and socialising in the evening in the house when the weather draws in more.

The lighting of the Rayburn and having a constant hot oven with trays of roasted vegetables helped keep morale high, and as we approached the final week before the film crew returned I rallied the volunteers and productivity increased. When Kevin McCloud returned, there was a finished house. The final filming went well, although it seems bizarre to have raised the house by hand, only to see a small crane arrive to raise the camera above the house. A large light was lifted up to simulate the moon, and that ended a rather surreal experience. As the film crew left, I found myself with a few moments to absorb the immensity of what happened that year. I sat on the veranda and I felt proud. This creature has built his nest. The next day I began coppicing.

*   *   *

The following spring was the first showing of the *Grand Designs* programme and the Lickfold Inn had a special screening. A good number who had been involved with the build and a large number of villagers turned up. We watched the show and then enjoyed a spontaneous party to follow. The show generated a huge amount of interest, far more than I could have imagined. It was discussed both on *Wogan* and *This Morning* with Richard and Judy, and I was soon being asked for magazine and press interviews. This dose of instant 'fame' did not sit comfortably with me, and I was glad to have the grounding influence of Prickly Nut Wood to keep me focused on what was real and important.

Grand Designs filmed two further programmes with me, a re-visit and a second re-visit, bringing the viewers up to date with an extension and the additions to my family. The second re-visit I agreed to do, providing I was given the opportunity to explain a little more about the coppicing process. The producer agreed, and the importance of the woodland and its management was put across to the viewer.

Grand Designs that year had a large '*Grand Designs* Live' show in London, and this was televised throughout the week. It involved a public vote and my house was voted the best all-time Grand Design – Kevin McCloud made no secret that he agreed with the verdict. Such attention to a house that I built on a low budget and wanted filmed purely as an educational tool was not at all what I had expected. My house had become a personality. People in the street would ask me, 'How is the house?' as if it had feelings or they were asking me about my children. I soon received enquiries asking whether I would build houses for other people. It was a route I believe I wisely avoided for a few years. The experience of building your own house was massive enough, especially when it had taken almost 10 years of basic living before I got permission. But to then have your house magnified in the public imagination into becoming this iconic building meant I needed time away from thinking about further builds – and anyway I had woods to manage.

I continue to get many letters and emails, some of which were beautiful explanations of what the house and the process I had been through meant to people. On some level I touched a latent part of the human psyche through this building, and it became a common thread that the correspondence contained the words 'I was in tears watching your programme.' I fought long and hard about what it was that had affected people to such a deep level. Possibly it was the reality of my situation – I was living in a caravan with a leaky roof and I was building a home, a shelter I really needed. So many episodes of *Grand Designs* seem to be about throwing large sums of money to build a dream house; many people on the show spend far more on a kitchen than I did on the entire house. But what I feel really happened was the woods and the woodland way of life unlocked something in people. Maybe it was related to the instinct I mentioned above, that there was something instinctual in my house and Prickly Nut Wood that people understood and wanted to experience. It may be that modern life has removed us from our natural instincts and parts of us crave the simplicity of living closer to nature. For the past eight years I have run four ticketed open days each year. These are usually booked up to six months to a year in advance, and the continued demand never ceases to amaze me. People come to experience the house but what they don't realise is that the house is a very small part of their visit to Prickly Nut Wood. I take them deep into the woods, immerse them in the management of the coppice, and when they eventually get to see the house they realise the building itself is a by-product of the woodland management. I think that makes the experience of the house that much more tangible.

*   *   *

For the past 14 years I've taken on apprentices at Prickly Nut Wood, and they live and learn the woodland lifestyle. Part of their training, once they've learned to cut the coppice, cleave poles and understand the wildlife management of the woods, is to learn the jointing techniques of roundwood timber framing. One year my apprentices Dylan and Rudi were so keen on the framing they asked me if I could find them building work. I had been approached by Pestalozzi International Village, who wanted a small barn constructed for an organic garden scheme. This seemed a good project on which the apprentices could gain some experience and for me to see how they got on. They excelled on the framing and the pretty barn we constructed at Pestalozzi was admired by many. I was then approached by Chris and Lucy Wall-Palmer, char-coal burners from Midhurst, who were putting in for planning permission and wanted to build a house in a similar style to my own. That autumn we constructed the frames of the house, and Chris then took on the rest of the build and has constructed a fine house for his family. With the increase in build-ing projects and the need to comply with legislation, I set up the Roundwood Timber Framing Com-pany Ltd, to facilitate the building of roundwood timber-frame buildings and to train new people in the techniques involved.

The increase in building projects has got me to tailor a lot more of my coppice management to the needs of the roundwood timber-framing company and its projects. For example, new products I now source from the coppice include: roundwood framing poles for our projects and for other people; round-wood wind braces; split chestnut lath; split chestnut shingles; split hazel and chestnut for woven panels in the buildings for earth plaster or beneath handrails. Much of the wood sourced from standard trees in the coppice is converted on a mobile sawmill to produce cladding, veranda floorboards and window seats for placing on top of straw-bale walls. Bale spikes for securing straw bales are another product that has evolved as a result of the demand for roundwood buildings. These materials I mention are predominantly from sweet chestnut coppice, but I have also been sourcing materials from plantations to use for frame construction. I believe there is a good market for larch, Douglas fir, Lawson cypress, Scots pine and western red cedar for roundwood timber framing projects.

These plantations are managed on a clear-fell regime, as mentioned in Chapter 3. This practice involves a first thinning, a second thinning, a third thinning, and then a clear fell. Depending on the species involved, it is about 40 to 70 years between planting and felling. The first two thinnings that are carried out are an economic loss; it is only the third thinning and the clear fell that bring in the economic return. For roundwood timber-framing poles, I am looking for plantations that have not been well managed. In other words, plantations in which the first and second thinnings have not occurred. This leaves tall, thin poles, whose growth rings are close together. These poles will be stronger in construction and will have long lengths, without having put on too much diameter. As this is a new market, trees have not been purposefully grown for this market, so I have had to rely on poorly thinned plantations. However, considering that the first and second thinnings provide an economic loss, it would make sense to plant some plantations of useful species for roundwood timber framing in which we leave the plantation un-thinned, saving the economic loss of early thinnings and subsequently removing poles for roundwood timber framing, which have a high value as a raw product. Although it is likely that removal at this time will cause some windthrown trees, many others will begin to put on girth and can then be converted by a mobile sawmill to floor joists, roof rafters and stud work for use in the roundwood timber-framing construction. The whole plantation can be grown to support the construction of new roundwood timber-frame buildings.

The Roundwood Timber Framing Company has constructed a number of other social and private buildings, including the highly acclaimed Lodsworth Larder, a community village shop, and winner of nine architectural and social enterprise awards to date. This shop is constructed from materials sourced primarily from a derelict coppice within the parish, which enabled an ancient woodland to be restored, such that in the following year it sent out a flush of violet helleborine orchids. The oak standards that were felled travelled fewer than three miles in total from the derelict coppice to the sawmill, where they were converted, air dried, then kiln dried, planed, and tongue and grooved, then returned to the building site to form the oak flooring. The construction of the shop involved the training of apprentices, and many villagers were involved in parts of the construction, as well as in the communal moving of the frames. The shop employs two full-time local staff and is supported by community volunteers. It carries out a number of community functions, from postal services and local information to ticketing for local events. It supports and supplies local foods and fresh produce, and has become an important meeting point and social hub within the village.

Another interesting Roundwood Timber Framing Company building is the Woodland Classroom at the Sustainability Centre in East Meon, Hampshire. This involved the felling of Lawson cypress from a plantation at the centre and moving the poles 200 yards to the building site. The building has an unusual curved roof that was formed by steam bending Lawson cypress poles for three hours each, and then setting them in a jig to create the shapes of the roof. A cordwood and clay wall forms the backdrop, in which a fireplace creates a focal point. A large decked area and canvas drop sides allow diverse use of the space.

Withyfield Cottage at Partridge Green in West Sussex is available for rent as an ecological holiday home and gives the public the opportunity to experience staying in a roundwood timber-frame house. Speckled Wood is a new training accommodation building constructed for the National Trust near Haslemere, Surrey. All the timber was sourced from the National Trust site at Blackdown where the building is situated, and it was featured on BBC's *Countryfile*.

There are now a significant number of roundwood timber-frame buildings constructed in the south-east, all checked by engineers and approved by building control. This gives great encouragement as to the viability of this technique. Ex-apprentices are building a house in Cornwall, and I am in contact with people all around the globe constructing roundwood timber-framed houses in their different localities.

So I found a niche in the woodland market, helped without doubt by the popularity of the *Grand Designs* documentary but solidified by a number of fine, sustainable buildings that have pleasing aesthetics, as well as good ecological credentials. As roundwood timber framing grows and spreads across the UK and globally, the opportunity for more woodland products to supply the building industry will increase and others will manage woodland to support the building industry of the future, which I believe will need to rely more on the local sourcing of its materials.

Roundwood timber framing uses local timber resources, and empowers people to take the initiative in building their own homes and community buildings. It leaves buildings that will degrade naturally, so that future generations will not have to deal with piles of non-biodegradable toxic materials when the buildings eventually reach the end of their lives.

When a roundwood timber-frame building is finished, the pile of 'waste' consists of wood off-cuts, which are then used to heat the building.

Roundwood timber framing shows it is possible to build ecological buildings that help support the management of sustainable woodland industries such as coppicing and, in doing so, offers a positive method of construction for our current generation without depleting the resources available for the next generation.

— CHAPTER SIX —

Trees of Prickly Nut Wood

With my home completed and a small construction industry of roundwood buildings starting to grow and spread under its own steam, I looked at Prickly Nut Wood with fresh eyes. I had used coppiced sweet chestnut for the roundwood frames of the buildings and although this has helped to stimulate the management of the chestnut woods and bring employment to others working in the woods, what of the other tree species that grow in and around Prickly Nut Wood?

Throughout the woods, there are a number of English oak (*Quercus robur*) standards that grow proudly above the coppice understory. These significant trees have grown large and dominant, and in many areas where the woods have not been worked for half of a century or more they have shaded out the diverse coppice below them. I mentioned earlier the connection I have with 'Shakespeare's Oak' that stands proudly over the chestnut coppice near to my house. As I have walked the countryside, I have admired oak trees of many sizes and forms. The large pollards and parkland oaks that stand out in the open landscape form strong markers throughout the English countryside. Not far from Prickly Nut Wood on the Cowdray Estate stands the Queen Elizabeth Oak, an ancient tree with a vast circumference, but diminished in height as it begins to shrink back into itself (as we all do when we reach the latter years of our lives). But although an oak may retreat for a few hundred years, its ageing process is extended way beyond our brief spell of life.

A pollard is the term used to describe a broadleaf tree that has been cut during the dormant (winter) season six foot (1.8m) or more above the ground. The tree sends up shoots in a similar manner to coppice but is cut at a height where animals cannot graze the re-growth of young shoots. Pollarded poles are cut on a rotation and used in a similar way to coppiced wood. Pollarding is mainly carried out on old trees for conservation purposes; the poles are generally used for firewood and cutting a tree at six foot off the ground is a more hazardous and time-consuming activity than coppicing, where the felling takes place at ground level. One product still used in craftwork from pollards is baskets made from riverbank pollarded willows.

The oak has been intimately tied up with our history and culture – from the wonderful hammer-beam trusses in Westminster Hall through to the solid cottage furniture that now sits in the windows of antique shops in the nearby town of Petworth – and our relationship with it has charted the growth of our civilisation. Oak, like sweet chestnut, contains the reserves of tannins that makes it such a durable timber, and one that for many centuries has been the first choice for buildings and for the ships we used in times when we exploited the lands of others for our gain.

From houses to ships, whisky barrels to church steeples, tables to charcoal, the oak tree has supplied our needs and the tannins from its bark has cured skins for our leather. To consider that such a monumental tree could be disappearing may be hard to contemplate, but our oaks are under attack more now than ever before. The pathogen known as *Phytophthora ramorum* that causes sudden oak death has attacked and killed many oaks in North America, and its arrival in England, where it is able to use rhododendron as a host plant, threatens our sturdy giants.

English oaks have, however, shown some resistance and the *Phytophthora* has jumped species and is now focusing on wiping out the Japanese larch (*Larix kaempferi*) plantations of Wales and south-west England. But our oaks are also under threat from defoliation. An increase in the number of caterpillars as a result of milder conditions seems to be one contributor, and although oak usually recovers with fresh leaf growth the following year, the stress and lack of growth, and the tree's inability to photosynthesise, will take its toll. The oak processionary moth (*Thaumetopea processionea*) arrived in 2006 from Central Europe. It not only attacks oaks, but the caterpillars have tiny hairs that are sharp, barbed and contain a toxin (thaumetopein) that causes irritation and allergic reactions in humans.

Oaks are not alone in suffering the risk of new diseases. Ash (*Fraxinus excelsior*) is under severe threat from ash dieback (caused by the fungus *Hymenoscyphus pseudoalbidus*), and many of our coniferous species are being attacked by one pathogen or another. I am astonished that we allow this to happen. These diseases have arrived in the UK, mainly by having been carried on plants we have imported, and possibly by unclean shoes and footwear carrying disease from forests in Europe across to the UK. I remember visiting Australia about 12 years ago and being impressed by the vigilant biosecurity measures, which involved spraying new arrivals to the country. Sadly, we've already let many diseases onto our island, but we must not hesitate from tightening up border controls and ensuring that we learn from the sensible and cautious precautions that are being used in countries like Australia.

As our oaks struggle to adapt to our changing climate, the trees themselves still need managing, and

in the derelict corpses around Prickly Nut Wood I often need to thin five or six standards per acre to reduce the canopy cover over the coppice to around 10 per cent. This extra light allows the regenerating coppice below to re-grow with vigour, and creates a more productive and biodiverse woodland. The oak standards are far from perfect timber trees and the ones I fell vary in quality. The soils at Prickly Nut Wood rarely suffer from shake, so the timber is usually sound and the bottom of the butt up to about 12 feet is often of good quality. The continual felling and re-growth of the coppice has ensured no side branches have disturbed the stem and hence once it becomes timber it has no knots. These good-quality bottom butts I mill up and put in stick to air dry for furniture making in the future. The next part of the stem is often also a timber log, but of poorer quality. Timber logs with a few knocks will be milled 'through and through' into planks and then air dried for about six months. After that they go to my local timber mill where the timber will be kiln dried into tongue-and-groove flooring that will be used in future buildings. Some of the trees will be milled into three-quarter-inch boards with a waney edge on one face, and these will form the cladding that is so characteristic of the rustic look for which roundwood timber-frame buildings are becoming so well known. The branches are corded up into lengths for firewood and charcoal production, and slowly the tree is processed and its presence removed from the wood. When felling a large oak, it is hard not to be impressed by the sight of the growth rings. I count them not just to age the tree, but also to follow the patterns of its growth. The gaps between the rings tell their own story – open to interpretation – of good and poor years of growth.

A coppice with standards woodland gives an extra layer in the woodland for wildlife, and oak standards will not only supply a nesting habitat for birdlife but, when old and hollow, for bats as well. These trees have also been recorded to support 284 insect species (423 if we include species of mite) and 324 associated species of lichens. It astonishes me to consider that one species of tree can offer the diversity to attract such a range of insects. It is similarly astonishing if we consider the abundance of ground flora below the tree in a well-managed coppice, and recognise that all this is obtained by managing a woodland for poles and timber from which, in turn, we can build houses.

As I restore derelict mixed coppice, the range of trees and finding the different uses that emerge is one of the pleasures of being a woodsman. Hazel (*Corylus avellana*) is the most traditional of coppice trees, and although not durable like sweet chestnut it has its own unique characteristics, such as the strength of its fibres that, when twisted, can form a strong, fibrous rope. This ability to be flexible and bend back on itself has meant hazel has for years been used for traditional woven products such as baskets, hurdles and the binders woven along the top of a freshly laid hedge. Historically, hazel was the 'go to' wood of the countryside when you needed material to make products. Every village would have contained areas of hazel coppice to meet those local needs. Herbert Edlin, in his excellent *Woodland Crafts in Britain*, mentions a statute passed by Edward IV in 1483 authorising the enclosure of woods for a term of seven years after cutting. With hazel being traditionally cut on a seven-year cycle, this protection of the re-growth shows the importance of the coppiced wood to rural industry. From hurdles to sheep penning, broches for thatching, pea-sticks, bean poles, faggots, a vast collection of animal and fish traps, etherings, walking sticks, hoops, feeding cradles and mangers, and crate rods for the potteries, hazel was an essential ingredient in day-to-day life. This regular seven-year harvesting of the coppice continued to produce a vast amount of poles, and in turn the ground flora of these coppice woodlands was establishing itself to become the gem of biodiversity that we see today.

Many of these traditional products have now been superseded by plastic alternatives, but plastic's victory is by no means universal. Materials for thatching and hedging are still sought for traditional uses, and the garden market has turned the sheep hurdle into rustic fences popular throughout the countryside. The attractiveness of its bark has encouraged a range of new obelisks and plant supports, making the garden a final destination for much of the hazel now being cut. The best-quality hazel coppice will not be found on the greensand and Wealden clay of the western Weald where I work the woods, but on the chalkland of Hampshire, Dorset and Wiltshire. I have seen some of the finest hazel in the country in Cranborne Chase and King's Somborne, and these patches are well guarded by coppice workers who know their true worth.

At Prickly Nut Wood, the hazel has been long neglected and it is only in recent years that I have begun the process of restoration. The coppice is mixed, and although there are large areas of hazel the quality will never attain that of the single-species copses growing on the chalk. My needs for hazel are mainly within the building and garden sectors. In roundwood timber-frame buildings, I use cleft hazel to weave a wattle frame to which I apply a layer of clay or lime plaster. I have also used the wattle to infill below the hand rails that enclose verandas, a popular feature on these buildings. In gardens I make woven panels, using chestnut posts and rails to create a durable frame. I then split and cleave the hazel to infill the panel.

4 February

Cold and still morning. I ventured up into Captain's Wood. Here the frost was still clinging to the hazel stems despite the welcome warmth of the winter sun penetrating through the woodland. I brushed past the yellow catkins and noticed the dust cloud of pollen. I looked closer, tapping the catkins and watching the pollen spread. As I focused in further, I noticed a small crimson flower that I had not seen before. The female flower of the hazel tree is so well hidden it is easy to miss. With my eye tuned to the colour I looked closer and more flowers appeared from out of their hiding places. How much more there is to see when I slow down and look ...

I cut the hazel first. With so many standard trees in close proximity, the hazel has sent out long stems high into the canopy in order to survive. These stems have twisted and turned wherever necessary to find their way through the darkening cover above them to a small glimmer of light. This has been the survival strategy of the hazel in this wood, and without it all the coppice stools would have died. 52 years have passed since it was last cut and the tangled growth makes it difficult to re-coppice. Many of the stems are entwined with other trees, and each one needs to be pulled and twisted free. Cutting hazel this old and derelict is a challenging task. Once the hazel is all down, the woodland is clearer and it is easier to make out the other species of trees and work out their felling directions. First, though, the hazel must be sorted. The thicker stems of four to eight inches in diameter are cut to six-foot lengths for firewood. The straightest poles for cleaving are bundled up, and some long hazel poles are chosen for a cooper from Liverpool who makes hoops for barrels for the Tower of London. A few walking sticks stand out and are leant against a large oak. Bean poles are bundled up and pea sticks placed to one side. Even out of poor-quality derelict coppice there are products to be had. The rest of the brash, too twisted for faggots, is burnt, creating a good winter's fire for our regular baked-potato lunches.

The rest of the felling will be in two parts. First, the mixed coppice of assorted sizes, then the thinning of the oak standards. The long coppice cycle has favoured ash trees in the wood and there are many tall, long stems to be cut. With a base diameter of between six and twelve inches, there will be some good timber from these trees. Ash is well known in Sussex as the 'widow maker'. Some say this is because it can drop branches, but I have always known it is because of the felling. If one is not careful, ash has a habit of splitting from the felling cut upwards. With a large, overstood coppice stool, felling needs to be all the more carefully done. About twenty years ago I felled a small copse at the foot of Blackdown, near Prickly Nut Wood. One afternoon the owner, a pathologist, came down to see how I was getting on. He told me – rather insensitively, I thought – that he had just done a post-mortem on a forester who had been killed by a tree springing back on him while felling. Once the pathologist had left the wood, I looked at the overstood ash coppice I was felling and went home early that day. The widow-maker commands respect.

Ash grows well in most soils but thrives best in soils above limestone. It coppices well and self-seeds, and is also found as a standard above hazel coppice. As a standard, it is better silviculturally than oak as it casts a dappled shade and is usually the last tree to come into leaf, allowing the underwood beneath a head start. Although ash is non-durable in the ground, it has the wonderful quality of being able to withstand shock and vibration, and has been, and still is, used for such purposes. It is used for tool handles, vehicle timber (in the Mini Clubman and Morris Minor Traveller), and all types of sporting equipment: cricket stumps, hockey sticks, billiard cues and the hurley used in the Irish sport of hurling. What other wood could survive the impact generated in the game of hurling? The hurling sticks are chosen from the base of the ash tree. This is the strongest part of any tree, as the stem disappearing down into the roots is always the hardest to split with an axe. It has grown strong supporting the weight of the main trunk as it blows in the wind. Ash is the usual wood for making scythe handles and hay rakes, and traditional green-wood chairs have been made from coppiced ash. Most of these products have been cleaved from the round and then worked to the desired shape from a quartered piece of timber in order to gain maximum strength and avoid splitting. Today ash is still the favourite chair-making wood

amongst most green-wood workers I have met. Fast-growing and straight-grained, it cleaves easily and is a pleasure to work with a draw knife or chisel. It steam-bends well and the finished look is attractive, with its pale colouring ready for any finish one might choose to add. As I write this I am sitting on a ladder-back ash chair made by one of my apprentices, Mark Krawczyk, on a course with Mike Abbott, a renowned chair-making teacher in green-woodworking circles.

I utilise ash in roundwood timber framing. The strength of the timber makes it very useful for wind or knee braces, helping control any movement (racking) of the building. I also enjoy burning ash logs, and always save a few for burning on special fires over Christmas and throughout the coldest nights of winter. Ash is a popular fodder for the deer population, so I need to re-fence the coppice before the re-growth begins. Every year at Prickly Nut Wood, we make up replacement tool handles and I have a fine long-handled fork and spade made from a strong quartered-stem ash by Thomas Baker, a past apprentice. Gate hurdles are often made from ash, but with the abundance of sweet chestnut growing at Prickly Nut Wood, I choose the more durable chestnut every time.

Another tree that appears in the mixed coppice I am cutting is silver birch (*Betula pendula*). Although not recommended as a coppice tree, it will coppice successfully if cut when young. Once the stems have grown beyond 12 inches in diameter it often dies during the coppicing process and rarely re-shoots. However, this does not mean that the birch is lost. Its ability to self-seed is astonishing and any clear area in the woodland quickly turns into a forest of emerging young birch saplings. Whilst in the south-east of England I am spoiled by a large selection of tree species with particular uses, birch – with its ability to grow in cold and harsh climates – has been used for a wide range of products. In the highlands of Scotland, Scandinavia and northern Russia, there is little else to use. Furniture, wooden shoes, chairs, tables and a variety of kitchen treen (tools) can all be made from birch. The timber is not durable and soon rots if in contact with water or the ground, with only the durable birch bark remaining. If it is off the ground and kept dry from the weather, however, the timber will survive well. The first roundhouse I built at Prickly Nut Wood about 16 years ago has birch logs as part of the cordwood wall. With a good roof overhang the timber has stayed solid and, from seeing this, I can understand why it was used in construction in northern climates. At Prickly Nut Wood I am spoilt with durable timber such as sweet chestnut, and so mainly use birch for firewood. It burns hot and bright, and, when mixed with a slower-burning wood, it creates a good fire. I use birch bark for fire-lighting. It remains by far the best of all fire-starters I have found in the woods. In many cultures the bark is used for a range of craftwork, from building canoes to covering furniture. Sheets are cut and peeled from the tree, and these are then used like a wallpaper to leave the beautiful bark pattern as a finish upon a dresser or wardrobe. Our birch in the UK is rarely of a quality from which to peel large sheets, but smaller items can be crafted from this beautiful bark. My other use of the silver birch is – along with sycamore and field maple – to tap it for wine. The collection of sap is a spring activity enjoyed by many in the woods.

7 March

A fine morning. Crisp frost, with the first signs of the sun flickering through the trees. Yesterday I snapped a small branch on the young birch and sap began to flow. So today I took my leather bag, filled with a drill brace and bit and a length of plastic pipe, and, carrying two glass demijohns, set off to tap the birch. I spent time choosing my trees, looking for ones of at least nine inches in diameter at the base and with a smooth bark. I found two near the pond. They are at the edge of the wood, so they get the morning sun. I placed the demijohns on the ground in front of the tree and measured with my length of pipe the height where I needed to drill the hole. I chose the southern side of the tree, as it will get the most sun, which will speed up the sap flow and process of collection. I insert the end of the bit at about 45° pointing upwards and begin to turn the brace. I cannot have been more than half an inch into the tree before the flow of sap begins to drip. I insert the pipe into the hole and seal round the edge of the pipe with clay. I sit and stay for a while, watching the increasing pace of the drips as a puddle begins to form in the bottom of the demijohn. I feel awakened from the long nights of winter, privileged to be collecting the essence of spring in my demijohn …

Throughout Prickly Nut Wood there are both natural streams and drainage ditches facilitating the flow of water off the hill above. Where these run deep through the copse, alder (*Alnus glutinosa*) has made its home. Alder is a water-loving tree, and will thrive in damp and at times waterlogged conditions. It is fast-growing, and will seed freely when given space and light, and therefore develops well in a mixed coppice such as I am working at Prickly Nut Wood. Alder has the useful property of absorbing nitrogen from the air and fixing it in root nodules through a relationship with the ascomycete fungus *Frankia alni*. The nitrogen is then drawn up through the leaves, and when the leaves fall in autumn and decompose the nitrogen is made available to other species through soil enrichment. Alder is a successful coloniser, its seeds having tiny floats that enable them to drift downstream until they are washed ashore, where they will then grow.

Alder was used for the making of clog soles, and the woods used to be full of cloggers who supplied the factories and workplaces of the industrial revolution. Alder wood has the ability to cope with moisture, and with the transition from being wet to dry that would split many other types of wood. It was favoured for this quality throughout the north of England, the Scottish lowlands and many parts of Wales.

I use alder mainly to make charcoal. Alder makes a good charcoal, and as it often grows in inaccessible areas from which timber is difficult to extract, it makes sense to convert it to charcoal and carry the charcoal out of the woods. Charcoal weighs about a fifth of the weight of the original timber. Gunpowder manufacturers rated alder charcoal very highly and, having compared it with other timbers I have converted into charcoal, I can see why. The end product is a shiny, smooth charcoal that holds together well and doesn't break up as easily as some woods that I have converted. It lights easily and is a fine, marketable product. One of the delights of cutting alder is the rich orange colour that the wood develops as the cut face is exposed to the air. A stack of freshly cut alder logs on the side of the ride cannot be mistaken for any other timber. However, over time the colour fades and the timber blends back in to the more neutral colours of the woodland landscape.

Goat willow (*Salix caprea*) will join alder in colonising the damp areas and stream banks in the mixed coppice. Although of little value as timber, its value comes in its early flowering, providing the first tree pollen for the bees to start harvesting. Woodlands provide a range of pollen for bees throughout the year, and at Prickly Nut Wood the bees begin with the goat willow, then move on to the blackthorn and plum. Pears and apples follow, and then soft fruits, wild blackberry, lime trees and chestnut. Ivy, with its late flowering, produces the last flush of woodland pollen. All of this is, of course, interspersed with flower pollen in the garden, and the clover that grows throughout the adjacent fields.

One tree that is well established amongst the mixed coppice at Prickly Nut Wood is field maple (*Acer campestre*). Its coppice stools are venerable, and typical of these ancient woodland copses. I use the wood for walking sticks and rustic furniture making, and have made a small chair from its twisted stems. In spring, although slower-flowing than the birch sap, field maple can be tapped for wine. In autumn, the tree stands out like a goddess clothed in a golden dress. The autumn colours of the field maple are perhaps the finest of any of our native trees, and always bring a smile to my face on a crisp autumn morning.

There are a few coppiced hornbeam (*Carpinus betulus*) trees in the woods. These graceful, silver stems are often found grown as a single-species coppice in the heavy clay soils of the Sussex Weald. An extremely hard timber traditionally used for cogs and wooden screws, the weight of the wood freshly felled will put an extra layer of muscle on a woodsman's arms, although left for a year or two, it becomes surprisingly light. Leave it any longer, however, and it will begin to rot. I use it mainly to make charcoal and as firewood, and it is ideal for either of these markets. As a coppiced tree, it needs good protection as it is enjoyed by browsing deer. Because it is so slow to re-grow from the coppiced stool, it can take four or five years to get above deer-grazing height.

Another tree in the mixed coppice is hawthorn (*Crataegus monogyna*). Although I have made jelly and wine from the haws, it is not often I harvest them, but I enjoy the fresh leaves in a May salad. Its timber is hard and I make mauls for striking chisels from it, for when we are timber framing.

Rowan (*Sorbus aucuparia*) is abundant throughout Prickly Nut Wood. It thrives on the damp acid soils and readily seeds itself. It grows to a good size, coppices well, and I have used the smaller thin stems to make rustic baskets and the odd walking stick. One characteristic of rowan I have observed is its unusual biological timing. It is often in flower and forming fruit before many other trees have broken leaf; likewise, it is usually the first to shed its leaves in the autumn. I make a wine from the berries and sometimes a jelly, which makes a fine addition to pigeon breast or venison.

There are a few established crab apples (*Malus sylvestris*) at Prickly Nut Wood and I have coppiced one of these in the cant of mixed coppice I am cutting.

This produces good hardwood for mallets and a fine scented timber for burning on a Christmas fire.

One or two wild service trees (*Sorbus torminalis*) appear amongst the coppice. These do not coppice and re-shoot from the stool. Instead, like cherry, they sucker from along the roots. The wood is popular in France for musical-instrument making, but I have never cut one down. I like them to grow on and produce the berries, which, when bletted in autumn, are a delicious fruit and our native alternative to the grape – awkward to pick, but worth the effort. Like apples, the seeds contain cyanide, so remember to spit them out! With its small, maple-shaped leaves, the wild service turns a rich coppery red in autumn and fully complements the mixed colours of the broadleaf woodland.

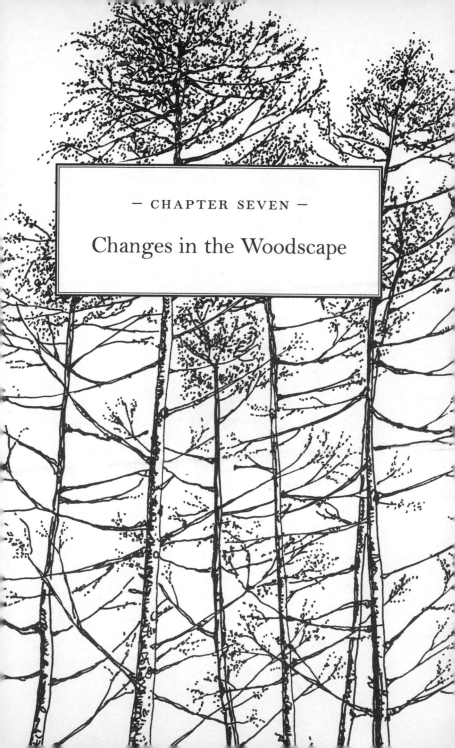

CHAPTER SEVEN

Changes in the Woodscape

One of the questions I am most often asked is about native species of tree versus exotic species, and whether we should only plant native. This is a complex question and, as with all questions regarding woodlands, we need to look at each woodland individually, assess it, and make a decision based upon that assessment.

Prickly Nut Wood is an ancient, semi-natural woodland and a Site of Special Scientific Interest (SSSI), although the dominant tree species, sweet chestnut, is actually an exotic brought in by the Romans. Chestnut has been in the UK for so long that it is often considered an honorary native, but I imagine for purists, a native tree is one that has grown in these islands since the end of the last ice age and has not been introduced by human beings. There are only 32 species of tree that satisfy these conditions.

Indeed, there are so many useful exotics that have been introduced over the last couple of hundred years, it would be hard to imagine not finding a place for them in our woodlands. Taking this into account, my thoughts are that I would first assess the woodland and see which species are already there. If it is an ancient woodland with a diverse native flora, then it is best not to add exotics. However, we have to be aware that if our climate continues to warm then the flora of our ancient woodlands will change, whether we do anything or not.

Take Bradfield Woods, with its wonderfully diverse ground flora. A rise in temperature could see many of these species migrating north to a cooler climate and more exotic species creeping in. If we can predict that the climate is going to get warmer and we are planting up new woodlands, then it certainly would be sensible to look at useful species that will grow well for the next generation in a slightly warmer climate. For suitable species for new woodland planting, I would be considering timber- and food-producing species, so I can envisage a potentially different emerging woodscape of mixed-species woodlands and agro-forestry systems designed for our anticipated needs in the future.

If we consider the south-east region where I am based, a rise in temperature would most likely see species such as beech moving northwards; even oaks might be on the edge of their climatic comfort zone. I have noticed an increase in the defoliation of oak trees, predominantly from caterpillar attack, and can only conclude that rising temperatures have improved conditions for caterpillars whilst increasing stress in oaks, making them vulnerable to such attacks. Sweet chestnut, because it originates in a Mediterranean climate, should thrive in any warming of the climate that occurs, provided that it is not attacked by blight or *Phytophthora*, which are causing such devastation to trees in the south-west of England such as Japanese larch. Sweet chestnut has natural durability and produces timber not dissimilar in quality to oak, but has the advantages of being faster-growing and producing a wonderful crop of edible nuts. I see sweet chestnut as an important timber tree in the south of England for the foreseeable future.

Another tree I would like to see more of in future plantings is the black locust (*Robinia pseudoacacia*). This species produces a very durable timber – again with similarities to oak – but, like alder, it also fixes nitrogen, so it could be a useful tree in mixed planta- tions. It coppices, suckers, and also produces flowers that are a good source of nectar for the bees. Its disadvantages are that it does not tend to grow very straight, has thorns and can be invasive, although I believe its invasive tendencies could be kept in check by the regular harvesting of poles.

An exotic tree I would recommend for damp conditions is the swamp cypress (*Taxodium distichum*). This species thrives in wet conditions and, being a deciduous conifer like larch, it loses its needles in the autumn, allowing the ground flora to survive beneath it. Swamp cypress produces a durable timber that is suitable for construction, and I can see no other tree that we currently grow in wetland areas that possesses that property. Willows and alders love damp conditions but neither are durable. One interesting silvicultural experiment would be to plant swamp cypress using alder as a nitrogen-fixing nurse crop. The fast-growing alder should help draw up the swamp cypress, producing good-quality construction poles and timber from the latter. This type of planting would ensure some of our poorer wet landscapes would produce useful timber to help meet the construction needs of future generations.

When choosing suitable trees that will thrive in our changing climate, we also need to be sure that the end product – the timber – will be of use to future generations. We should therefore be choosing species that have natural durability and strength. Douglas fir, European larch, Lawson cypress and Western red cedar are all species that fit this category, and if we were to plant them we would be leaving a heritage of trees useful for construction to future generations. Sweet chestnut, walnut, ash, black locust and hazel could form a useful selection of broadleaved trees that would leave future generations with a variety of timber for a multitude of purposes.

There is little doubt that our woodscape *will* change. It was not that many years ago that elm was a dominant forestry tree across our landscape, but now, with the exception of the streets and parks of Brighton, it is only noticeable as a hedgerow tree that dies back again once it reaches about six inches in diameter, as Dutch elm disease strikes again. The warming of our climate will gradually change our woodland species, with some trees and plants migrating north, while others will arrive from the continent. These changes will be gradual, but it is important that we act now and begin to plant useful species for future generations.

*   *   *

I believe agro-forestry will have a more important role to play in the future. Combined land-use systems, based on the principles of permaculture design, can create farms and landscapes that recycle nutrients and energy within farm systems, leaving healthier soils with established crops for the next generation to inherit. A large number of our current vast arable farms will leave little but barren fields devoid of much of their topsoil and dependent on massive inputs of fertiliser to grow the next crop. Leaving a landscape in such poor condition is detrimental to the health of generations to come, and the process of replenishing soil fertility needs to begin now if we are not to leave a poisoned chalice for those to come.

Agro-forestry systems can take many forms. Silvi-pastoral systems, such as those I have established on some farms near Prickly Nut Wood, are a traditional system of fruit trees grown as standards above a diverse grassland that is grazed by sheep or geese and other poultry. These systems produce a joint yield from the different components, and are labour-intensive if run well. I see the need for more labour as a benefit, as I believe future generations will be glad to find more work on the land. Growing food in this country will become the essential industry it once was. It was an arrogant colonial policy in the

Victorian era that we felt it was no longer necessary to grow all of our own food in the UK, and that imported foods were cheaper and would help to sustain us. Without aviation fuel, how are we going to fly beans in from Kenya? Other agro-forestry systems will involve nut trees over arable crops, and light shade-casting trees such as ash (or birch, if ash proves impossible to grow as a result of ash dieback) are likely to be seen more often, grown as firewood avenues between vegetable and cereal crops. Martin Crawford's work at the agro-forestry research trust in Devon gives us a real insight into the varieties of nut trees that will grow well in the future. The heart-nuts (*Juglans ailantifolia* var. *cordiformis*) Martin is growing are particularly impressive. They might offer better yields in the future and be grown successfully on a wider range of soils than more traditional walnut varieties.

I anticipate future generations will be less wasteful with wild animals, and especially those that predate upon crops, than our generation has been. We cannot separate growing nuts without controlling squirrels. The two are intrinsically linked, just as rabbits need to be kept out of vegetable crops and deer out of coppices. Any cultivation of nuts will involve the controlling – and eating – of grey squirrels. Future

generations are likely to inherit a good population of wild boar. The numbers have been growing steadily over the past ten years and in another thirty years I anticipate them being a regular feature in the wood-scape. A valuable source of food, they will need sustainable cropping to keep numbers in balance and supply boar for the table.

Another meat I anticipate future generations to eat is horse. I ate horse once in Norway and it had a fine flavour. Much of the grassland that surrounds me in West Sussex is managed purely for horses. Only in rare cases do any of these useful draught animals actually pull a cart or plough a furrow. Most of them are pleasure horses and, particularly around Prickly Nut Wood, there are acres of good productive land given over to polo ponies. I have nothing against polo as a game, but we cannot sustain such a vast number of ponies purely for our sporting indulgence on land that should be used for growing food or timber. I anticipate the decline of polo ponies running in parallel with the decline in the availability of petrol and diesel, and expect during my lifetime to be eating a polo pony or two.

One area where agro-forestry can play an important role is in towns and cities. For too long we have avoided planting fruit- and nut-producing trees as street trees because of our concern about fruit staining the paintwork of cars. It is time to re-prioritise what is important, and the time for choosing tree species to suit the habitat of the motor car is over. Avenues of sweet chestnut, walnut, pecan, almond, cherry, plum, pear and apple trees should become the future of our streets. Tree crops are perennial; once established, fruit and nut trees will produce well with little maintenance and most are able to cope with drought conditions. Imagine a city in which children can forage on the way to school. The use of agro-forestry could expand into parks and wastelands. The more trees we can plant in and around cities, the cleaner the air will be and the more pleasant they will be to live in. If we choose fruit and nut trees, the volume of perennial food grown in and around the city will greatly increase. Fruit and nut trees are good sources of nectar for bees and, in turn, the bees' pollination ensures good crops of fruit, so the expansion of rooftop beehives and more urban honey would be another benefit if these species were planted.

The resurgence in allotments and the desire to grow food again are truly positive aspects of our realisation of the need to engage with the land and begin to re-establish local systems of food and resources. We know that in times of extreme measures we are able as a people to respond to a crisis, as the 'Dig for Victory' campaign showed during the Second World War. However, we should not be waiting for a crisis to arrive. We should be putting in place the mechanism and plans to create sustainable systems for the next generation. Cities can utilise not just the streets and wastelands but also the vast acreage of vertical space for growing food, as well as rooftops. Food-production systems on vertical walls and rooftops should become part of the design of any new urban buildings.

Large-scale projects for resource management should be put in place, such as the management of land alongside our vast network of railway lines, to produce coppiced timber for fuel and power, and utilising the railway network to transport this timber would be a sensible use of resources.

One major change I expect to see is a move back towards more physical labour. We have a large population, and many people need work. Land-based work

is physical, and generally keeps people fit and in good health. The last 100 years have seen an oil-based economy in which machines have replaced people. But as oil becomes increasingly scarce and its price increases, people will have to begin to replace machines. I expect to see more community and cooperative groups managing both woodlands and agricultural land. Community-supported agricultural systems (CSA), in which people offer their labour and become involved in growing food on farms, in return being rewarded with agricultural produce, is a model that is likely to catch on and spread. Similarly, community-supported forestry (CSF), in which people trade their labour in a forest project for logs, bean poles or timber, would be a good model to further explore.

At Prickly Nut Wood, I run my apprenticeship scheme on similar lines. Apprentices trade their unskilled labour in return for training, accommodation and basic food. As their skill level increases, they receive payment for specific jobs. This may be in timber or in money. After about nine months to a year they are ready to head out and manage a woodland themselves. They then begin to regenerate other coppices and supply more timber products into their local market.

There are many good training courses provided by agricultural colleges, but nothing can replace practical placement within the land-based industries themselves. One of the difficulties for young people setting themselves up in forestry and agriculture is the cost of acquiring land – and, even more, the cost of accommodation. The coppice worker or vegetable grower is unlikely to earn enough in their enterprise to pay for the rental of an expensive rural cottage. The need for low-impact housing solutions for those working on the land has never been clearer. Rural areas need local workers producing food and resources, yet many of our farms have been separated from the farm-building infrastructure that they need in order to operate effectively. Prickly Nut Wood and the adjacent woodlands I manage would once have been part of Snapelands Farm. The barns at Snapelands would have been available for the processing of coppice produce and the storage of logs and materials. With the barns having been converted into dwellings and the majority of the land separated from the original farmhouse, I am left to run a woodland business without any infrastructure to manage the resource. Hence I have needed to build a house, barn and sheds to re-establish a woodland farm, a central hub to my working life and business that ensures the woodlands and associated management have a future. All over the countryside barn conversions are causing similar problems. As a barn is sold off and converted, the land is left without the infrastructure needed for its management. The next person to farm the land will no doubt need to build a barn. This is another area in which good planning guidance would encourage young people to live and work on the land. The current planning policies make it very difficult to achieve such aims.

Our woodlands are going to change over the next generation, as a result of climate change, disease, and the human need to plant and utilise the resources we need. Forestry is likely to become less mechanised and the amount of human labour used will increase, in both community groups and the private sector. It is our responsibility to honour these changes, putting in place the necessary woodland infrastructure and species choice for the next generation to thrive.

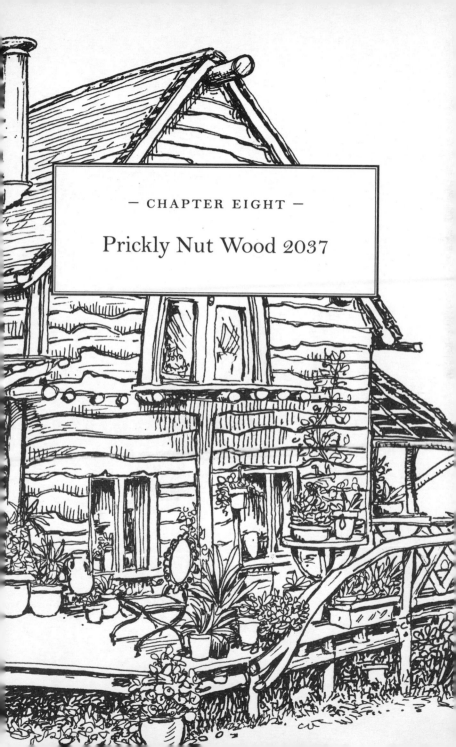

— CHAPTER EIGHT —

Prickly Nut Wood 2037

I take the familiar walk up the steps to join the old bridleway and head south through the rusty metallic gate towards Redlands Farm. I remember the farm as a dairy farm, but like many of the estate farms it was divided up after the oil crisis as part of the land-reform policy, and is now a number of smaller holdings. I walk through the farmyard and pass the redundant slurry tank. The field in the valley towards Smithbrook is now full of timber-frame caravans. I started making them for the national park back in 2013 and they really caught on. Their visual appearance – and the fact that they utilised local resources and labour to create a needed product – made them desirable objects. When Lodsworth became one of the re-settlement villages we built sixty of them, and they make a pretty picture, rather like an overgrown allotment whose sheds have expanded into wooden caravans with gardens all around them. Re-settlement villages provide temporary homes for those making the transition from urban to rural life. Most individuals or families are expected to stay a year or two before moving out to some of the new holdings that were drawn up after the land divisions, but there are a few like Tom and Angie who have been here longer. I hope they will be able to take on some land in the parish, and it would be a shame to see them go, as they are so much part of village life now.

I pass the old walnut tree in the field corner. I remember when I knew the few producing trees in the

parish. Now there are a few hundred walnuts and heartnuts. We did well here, getting so many fruit and nut trees planted before the oil crisis occurred. I take the track up past Bailey's yard to the power station.

The wood-fuelled power station was installed in 2017 and was one of a number of pilot small-scale power stations set up across the national park. It powers the village and often has surplus energy, but it takes a lot of organisation and labour to keep it going. The woodlands around Prickly Nut Wood and beyond easily supply enough timber, but the speed of cutting is slow. I cut most of the timber by hand now, double-handed cross-cut saws for the larger trees, and bow-saws and axes for the smaller ones. I have an electric chainsaw that is still working well, which I run off the solar panels when I do the cross cutting. My battery chainsaws have long since worn out. Lithium is no longer obtainable, and sourcing the parts for the majority of my power tools is a thankless task. Many are no longer available.

The timber is transported to the power station by horse. There are twelve village horses – four are Ardennes, and the rest are cobs of one cross or another. These are all working horses, owned by the parish for work on the land and in the woodlands. They are ridden for pleasure on occasion, but time for such luxuries is rare. After the oil crisis, most horses were eaten, and only those with the ability to work survived. Allowing for lameness or pregnancy, twelve horses seems to be about the right number for the village. There are nearly always at least two working at the power station, and a couple in the woods and on the land, leaving six for private activities amongst parishioners, the moving of re-settlers, weddings, funerals and deliveries. Their main grazing is up at Vinings, close to the power station and out of the main growing area to the east of the village.

I emerge up at Vinings and look across to the South Downs. So much is unchanged from the time before the oil crisis. It is certainly quieter, with the lack of motor cars and air traffic. The roads are almost empty, save for a few electrical cars belonging to doctors and peacekeepers, and the hydrogen buses that form the basis of the main transport link across the country. Bicycles are abundant again and the waterways are seeing active service. Many of the old canal routes have been re-opened, and all large industrial works are based around the river network. Steam power has had a small renaissance and is in use once again on the railways, proving to be more reliable than the remaining electric trains. The country's nuclear power stations are still producing energy, although a couple of reactors are being shut down, so the supply is irregular and when demand is high in the winter, long power cuts across the country are common.

My route takes me past the village hall and the school we built back in 2017. The school has 108 children and they work on the new curriculum. Half of their time in school is spent learning English, maths, science, history and computer programming, and the other half working on projects for the parish. Land-based skills are nationally recognised as essential, and survival beyond school without sufficient skills to work on the land will soon prove impossible. I teach at the school one afternoon a week – coppicing and craft skills during the winter, and roundwood timber-frame construction in the summer. The school is a roundwood timber-framed building, so the children see the structure and the jointing techniques every day. Practical sessions are always developed around creating something that is needed within the parish community, and we have been building a new caravan for the re-settlement area over the summer.

When children leave school they do two years' community service between the ages of 15 and 17. This involves parish maintenance of roads, tracks and buildings, and work in the fields, the power station

and wherever there is need for labour at that time. Every resident of Lodsworth, whether long-term or from the re-settlement area, must work in community service one week out of every four. This ensures that everyone contributes to meeting the parish's needs, and that seasonal tasks requiring extra labour are easily met. As most work tasks are shared, there is a strong sense of working together, and the village has developed a fine range of songs that are often heard on the wind when particular tasks are being carried out. Most work has a community benefit, but entrepreneurism is not discouraged, and although it is possible to build up individual wealth through trading and hard work, few people want to be seen to be doing that. The problems caused by bankers are still fresh and raw in most people's minds.

I pass the gnarled and twisted chestnuts, and head down the drive to Lodsworth House. It is bustling with activity, and I join in with the sorting and stacking of apples. Lodsworth House has become the main apple store and root cellar. The village has acres of orchards and, although much is made into its now famous cider and traded with other villages, a large number of apples are stored for winter and spring consumption. The house looks unchanged from the exterior, but the wire, rat-proof cages and the parish administrative offices inside the building betray its change in function. Only the offices have any form of heating; the rest of the building is kept naturally cool to help the preservation of the stored fruit and vegetables. Inside Lodsworth House, the smell of apples is pervasive, and the cages, with their trays of apples marked with varieties and dates, look well organised. Our food organisation has really improved over the last few years. Necessity dictates good work. The cider store is fairly empty, but pressing will begin in earnest over the next few weeks. Most of the poorer-quality village apples that will not store are graded out for cider, although some are reserved for apple juice. This mixed cider is called 'Lodsworth Standard', now a well-known drink across Sussex. The better-quality reserve cider is made from the orchards of single-variety cider apples such as 'Kingston Black', 'Crimson King', 'Harry Masters Jersey' and 'Yarlington Mill'. These are carefully looked after and brought out for celebratory occasions, of which there are a growing number.

With its return to being a more land-based community, Lodsworth celebrates the traditional seasonal festivals. The solstices and equinoxes are turning points in the day/light calendar that have become increasingly relevant when working on the land, and the marking of these occasions is well attended by the majority of the parish. Dancing and traditional Sussex songs have returned, as well as a number of good musicians who come together to form makeshift bands for these occasions.

Back in Lodsworth House, I head up to the parish administrative offices and register the number of boxes and varieties of apples harvested on my holding. I have arranged to take 'Haspen', a sturdy cob, together with his cart to collect the apples the following morning and transport them to the store. From the house I continue south, to the Langham Brewery. The brewery is a real asset to the village. Locally grown hops and barley have meant some recipes have had to change, but the quality of beer is recognised across the county and beyond. The brewery produces some fine pork from the Tamworth pigs living in the fields behind the brewery building that benefit from the spent grain from the brewery and the apple pulp from the cider pressings, which take place outside the Hollist Arms pub. The barrels are taken by horse-drawn dray along the roads for local deliveries, or taken down to Selham Quay, where the nimble barges head down the Rother to the Arun and beyond.

The bakery has expanded at Langham's stables and is now a bustling enterprise, ensuring the village is supplied daily with fresh bread. Seasonal recipes have developed and the abundance of walnuts makes a fine walnut bread, while in early spring the wild garlic ciabattas are eagerly anticipated. I stop for a pint at the brewery whilst discussing the number of chestnut poles that need to be cut this winter for the expansion of the hop gardens. I walk back up the main track to the village and pass the ever-bustling Hollist Arms. The pub – as well as the shop – is now owned and run by the parish, and this arrangement, which occurred with the community purchase prior to the oil crisis, has ensured the pub/shop combination is the focal point of village life. Much trading, discussion, banter, words of wisdom and utter rubbish are discussed, as would be expected in any good pub. The Hollist Arms has a wonderful history for me. I look back fondly to the days when Nick Kennard would leave a kitchen fork in the gutter by the back door and I would poke it through the keyhole, lift the latch, let myself in, help myself to a pint or two and settle up when he returned. Today, with the disappearance of the motor car, the use of the pub has greatly increased and a lunchtime pint is probably as popular as it was in the 1950s. I decline today, having already had a pint at the brewery, and go straight to the shop. Lodsworth Larder is a thriving hub of exchange and, since we expanded it in 2015, has become a trading post, not just for the supply of food and a wide range of domestic products, but acting as a go-between in sourcing some of the community's more unusual requests. Since the breakdown of the country's postal services, most unusual items are sourced on the Internet and delivered by an often slow and laborious route to a central drop-off point. In the case of Lodsworth, this is Lodsworth Larder. There is never a guarantee of delivery time, or in fact whether the item will be delivered at all.

Since the oil crisis, in Lodsworth we have been fortunate, as we had set up much of the infrastructure to deal with this moment. The localized power station, the vast orchards of fruit and nut trees we had planted and the established vegetable production to the north-east of the village put us in good shape; we were seen as a good example and chosen as a resettlement village for this reason. Seventeen years have since passed and although many aspects of life are as they once were, and in my mind better for the loss of the motor car and reliance on more local resources, there is still a cautious, unknown, uncertainty about the future. This may well diminish as those who were born since the oil crisis begin to take over the working of the land. Lodsworth is now a

thriving village of over 1800 residents, and as a resettlement village it has a rural medical outpost to deal
with the majority of medical needs. The rural medical
outpost has one emergency electric ambulance for
Lodsworth and surrounding villages.

I take the path through the cobnut platt and
continue along the edge of the Lod and then climb
towards Leggatt Hill. Through the vegetable gardens,
I pass by hedgerows being foraged for blackberries
and haws ready to make jams and wine. The richness
of our hedgerows and wild food is being appreciated
once again and children are growing up learning to
forage and work the land. Maybe the oil crisis was a
turning point, a reminder of what happens when you
lose your connection with the land and where you
come from and neglect to look after the needs of the
next generation.

I turn for home, across Lodsworth Common and
up the familiar track to Prickly Nut Wood. I look up
at the old oak, a beacon of calm throughout centuries
of human struggles. I sit beneath the tree and look
out across the coppice. The smoke from the outdoor
kitchen fire drifts across and I pick up the sound of
laughter from those around the fire. I hear a stag
bark in the distance, and I smile from deep within. 'I
know this place. I belong.'

Postscript

T his book is not meant to give answers to our environmental crisis and in particular the question of human survival on our planet. The answers to these uncertainties are incredibly complex, and human beings might only survive after disease or disaster has considerably reduced our numbers, forcing us to rethink our position as a species on this planet.

What I hope the journey I have shared will do is show that by acting now in a way that is responsible towards our resources, we are leaving our children with some hope as they grapple with the problems over resources that are awaiting them. Living in a world so dependent upon one main resource – oil – means that as it runs out, life as we currently know it will dramatically change. The greater the number of sustainable systems that are in place when it does run out, the easier the transition into a post-oil world will be. To me, it is easy to imagine rural settings in a post-oil economy, as it is those that I have the most direct contact and familiarity with. I do not doubt, however, that the urban situation will be the most challenging, and there will no doubt be overlapping migration in each direction.

If I take my own village of Lodsworth, there is clear evidence it has made some good steps towards being prepared for the challenges that lie ahead. The construction and opening of Lodsworth Larder, the community village shop, has created a trading point, an outlet and a local focal point for village life. The village pub next door keeps the supply of food and wines closely contained within the village. The opening of Lodsworth Larder as a retail outlet has both helped and encouraged local businesses to thrive. The village has its own brewery, the Langham Brewery, producing a fine range of beers, and acres of new vineyards have been planted on the southern slopes of the parish and are beginning to produce some excellent wines. A village baker produces a range of quality breads to supply to the shop, and fresh seasonal vegetables are supplied by a local grower, now looking to establish the vegetable-growing business in the centre of Lodsworth. All of these businesses have sprung up over the past few years and the community village shop has been the catalyst. Add to this my work in the surrounding woods, together with the type of infrastructure that will need to be in place post-oil, and our planning is already underway.

What is happening is that the local infrastructure of supplies of food and resources is already beginning to be put in place. This model can be expanded upon and reproduced all around the country to create healthy, vibrant communities that are taking responsibility to ensure a better way of life both now and for future generations. Lodsworth could be further improved by considering the feasibility of a small community wood-fired power station. Lodsworth is surrounded by woodland and could easily become self-sufficient in fuel. Its surrounding fields could be better utilised by turning some in to orchards and by producing more food. All of this goes against the trend of the large multi-national supermarkets that worm their way into small communities, extracting the hard-earned cash and resources from these communities which then disappears into the pockets of shareholders living in other parts of the world. Lodsworth Larder was set up as an industrial provident society, with the profits being returned to improving the infrastructure and needs of the village community. In other words, spend your money in your local shop and the profits will improve the environment in which you are living.

Town and country planners could do with enlisting the input of permaculture designers when they draw up local plans. Administrative boundaries are likely to become less important in a post-oil world, in which resource boundaries and river catchments should dictate development where necessary. New settlements can be built to help house our burgeoning population, but design needs to be led by available resources and future resource needs, not by how much space is needed to park large numbers of motor cars.

Our aim, wherever we live over the next few years, must be to build up the necessary infrastructure and resource base to enable us to be in the best possible position to deal with the changes post-oil society will bring. The work of the Transition Towns Movement is attempting to implement such plans and strategies at local level, and is a good place to start the process.

It is easy to feel very isolated as the juggernaut of oil-based economic development powers forward, seemingly unaware of the critical position of its fuel gauge. But every change, however small, in putting in place strategies for our future will make such a difference when that time comes.

One action that most of us as individuals can take, whether in the country or the city, is to plant a fruit or nut tree and tend it, so that it will produce well for the next generation. Every person who undertakes this simple yet satisfying act will be greatly improving this environment and ensuring the necessary extra supply of perennial food is underway. Others in groups might target their councils. Together they can work towards the introduction of edible varieties of street trees, the transformation of wasteland into productive land, the harvesting of domestic rainwater, and the generation of local markets for local produce, to name but a few. Putting positive solutions for future generations in place is an empowering way to survive the challenging times ahead.

Once we start on the positive route of thinking for the needs of the next generation, our decisions become more balanced, more long-term and more sustainable. Implementing such strategies should be at the forefront of decision-making. Our democratically elected governments are trapped within short-term, five-year plans. Unable to look ahead to the next generation, they are constantly locked in a cycle of trying to get re-elected, often blinded to the future of our country and its needs. A reformed House of Lords might become the house for the next generation, a house that proposes and puts in place policies that move forward to be implemented, no matter which political party is in place in the Commons or for how long they govern. These universal policies could help us to put in place the necessary infrastructure to cope with the huge changes that the end of the oil-based economy will bring.

And throughout all the changes and upheaval, the chestnut coppice keeps growing; the woods, static in their rooted certainty, continue to put on growth, preparing to supply both us and the following generation.

Tree Cycles

When I first felled you
I was a young man,
Eagerly I watched you crash to the ground
I only glanced at the hidden rings
No other had seen
I now stare at in middle age.

How many have you warmed through winter's
    cold
How many houses hold your limbs
Holding up roofs for those who never knew you
How many cattle have you penned within the
    field
How many have eaten from your table and sat
    upon your chair?

Next time I fell you will be my last
Not yours, you will see many others, young and
    headstrong
Middle aged and reflective, old and frail
All taking what you so freely give.

Ben Law (first published in
The Woodland Year, 2008)

Glossary

Bender: temporary home or shelter made from hazel branches and canvas covering

Binders: twisted binding between stakes on a laid hedge, usually hazel – also called 'etherings'

Brash: small branches from side and top of tree

Cant: a defined area of coppice, also regionally referred to as a 'panel'

Cleave: to split un-sawn timber by forcing the fibres apart along its length

Coppice: broadleaf trees cut during the dormant season producing continuous multi-stems that are harvested for wood products

Crown: the branches and top of the tree above the bole

Faggot: a tied bundle of small branches traditionally used to fire ovens, now used for riverbank restoration and coastal defence

Greenwood: freshly cut wood

In-cycle coppice: coppice that has been cut at regular intervals and is not overstood

Maiden: young single-stem tree that has not been coppiced

Mortise: a chiselled slot, into or through which a tenon is inserted

Overstood coppice: coppice that has not been cut for many years and is out of rotation for usual coppice produce

Permaculture: ecological design for a sustainable future

Pollard: tree that has been cut above animal-grazing height to allow repeated harvesting of poles from the crown

Pleachers: partially cut-through stems of hedges that are laid at an angle and continue to grow as the sap still flows

Ride: an access route through a woodland, often used for timber extraction

Rootstock: the root onto which a scion is grafted

Snedding: removal of side branches and top of a felled tree

Standard: a single-stemmed tree allowed to grow to maturity, commonly amongst coppice

Stool: the living stump of a coppiced tree from which new stems grow

Suckering: re-growth from existing roots of a tree after cutting

Tenon: the projecting end of a timber that is inserted into a mortise

Underwood: coppice woodland

Windblow: trees that have been toppled over by the wind

Yurt: a wooden-framed, transportable dwelling with canvas covering, originating in Asia and now found as a dwelling in woodland

Index

Ben's previous books:

The Woodland Way
The Woodland House
The Woodland Year
Roundwood Timber Framing

If you would like to find out more about Ben's books, products, the courses and open days he runs and much more, please visit: www.ben-law.co.uk